GUIDO DA SIENA

GUIDO DA SIENA

by James H. Stubblebine

PRINCETON, NEW JERSEY

PRINCETON UNIVERSITY PRESS

1964

To the Memory of my Mother

PREFACE AND ACKNOWLEDGMENT

Guido da Siena has always played an important part in the history of Sienese painting. Indeed, considering the fact that his Palazzo Pubblico *Madonna* was signed and dated 1221, it is not surprising that as time passed Guido emerged as the legendary founder of the Sienese school. But in modern times, as art historical criticism assumed a certain precise nature, old legends were less easily repeated. A systematic study of the problems has gradually led us to an awareness that Guido worked, rather, towards the end of the thirteenth century. Along with the gradual accretion of works attributed to Guido and his school, a clearer conception of Guidesque painting has evolved, so that much of the older criticism is only an historical curiosity today.

It is the aim of this monograph to assemble and explore all those works with which the name of Guido da Siena is associated. Not only is it possible to gain a new perspective on Guido's artistic achievement and on the nature of Guidesque painting but we can also obtain a better understanding of the origins of Sienese painting. Not the least benefit is the corollary insights we gain into related masters of the thirteenth century: Coppo di Marcovaldo, Cimabue, and Duccio.

My interest in Sienese painting goes back to Professor Opdycke's introductory art history course at Harvard years ago; it was nurtured through seminars with Richard Offner at the Institute of Fine Arts of New York University. Professor Offner gave enormous stimulus to my work on Guido da Siena and it would be difficult to measure my debt to him. His article on Guido remains a definitive study of the artist.

Stephen Ostrow offered me considerable help, for which I am much indebted, in solving the many problems of the arrangement and diagramming of the San Domenico Altarpiece. I would like to thank Richard Schiff for valuable suggestions in regard to a number of the drawings. Mrs. Henry W. Howell, Jr., and the staff of the Frick Art Reference Library have been unfailingly helpful with various problems. Edward Garrison has been of considerable help both with advice and photographs. Needless to say, his *Italian Romanesque Panel Painting* has been an indispensable tool in my study of Dugento painting. Enzo Carli of Siena has proffered assistance on a number of occasions. Gertrude Coor was always most generous with advice and appreciative of the problems involved in this study. Martin Eidelberg helped me with a number of research problems. His perceptive suggestions about the manuscript have immeasurably improved it throughout. I am also indebted to him for much good advice about the drawings and reconstructions in this book and for the execution of all of them.

I am grateful to Richard Offner, Rensselaer Lee, and Millard Meiss, who were good enough to read the manuscript. Moreover, I would like to express my sincerest thanks to Professor Meiss for his generosity in discussing a number of the problems with me. The assistance, always both objective and encouraging, of Harriet Anderson of Princeton University Press is much appreciated. Lia Schipper corrected and typed the manuscript with a devotion far exceeding ordinary duty.

The Rutgers University Research Council generously aided my work with several grants. The publication of the book has been supported by a grant from the Ford Foundation.

Acknowledgment for Photographs

Unless listed below, the photographs are reproduced by courtesy of the owner specified in the captions.

Alinari, Florence: Figs. 1, 2, 10, 31, 32, 35, 37, 40, 43, 55, 72, 74, 85, 86, 87, 88, 90, 92, 106, 107, 108, 110, 111, 112, 115, 121, 125, 126

Alinari-Anderson, Rome: Figs. 15, 39, 75, 76, 77, 78, 89, 105, 117, 127

Alinari-Brogi, Florence: Figs. 63, 64, 84

Croci, Bologna: Fig. 82

Frick Art Reference Library, New York: Figs. 42, 49, 104, 113

Gabinetto Fotografico Nazionale, Rome: Figs. 8, 24, 25, 28, 29, 30, 33, 41, 61, 65, 94, 103, 116

Garrison, Edward B.: Figs. 11, 12, 13, 34, 36, 123

Grassi, Siena: Figs. 14, 17, 19, 60, 65, 68, 70, 71, 83

Istituto Centrale del Restauro, Rome: Fig. 80

Lombardi, Siena (formerly): Figs. 3, 53, 100, 102, 114, 120

National Gallery, London: Fig. 128

Reali, Florence: Figs. 9, 66, 69

Soprintendenza, Florence: Figs. 7, 54, 62, 79, 81, 96, 97, 98, 99, 118, 119, 124

Staatliche Fotothek, Dresden: Fig. 27

From O. Sirén, *Toskanische Maler im XIII Jahrhundert*, Berlin, 1922, fig. 122: Fig. 95

CONTENTS

CONTENTS

ILLUSTRATIONS

PROLOGUE

PROLOGUE

The name of Guido da Siena does not appear in the great source of knowledge and legend about Italian art, the *Vite* of Giorgio Vasari. If he knew of Guido, who painted before such luminaries as Giotto and Duccio, and at roughly the same time as Cimabue, all of whom helped, as he saw it, to restore painting to its old glory, he kept his silence. The only thirteenth century painter granted a *Life* is Margaritone d'Arezzo but he appears only by way of doing honor to Vasari's home town. Had Margaritone been a Sienese, he too would surely have gone unmentioned.

It is hard to imagine that Vasari, who must have canvassed the cities and towns of Italy with uncommon thoroughness in his search for the art of the past, would not in the very ordinary course of events have seen some of the works of Guido and his shop, especially the great *Madonna* (Fig. 14), now in the Palazzo Pubblico of Siena, which was in the Capacci Chapel of San Domenico throughout the sixteenth century. But, of course, all such works would have proclaimed themselves to be part of the despised *maniera greca* and would by their very nature have appeared indistinguishably anonymous. To identify a particular painter of the thirteenth century would militate against the thesis Vasari propounds in regard to Cimabue and Duccio and Giotto and, indeed, would go against his notion of the individual, famous artist, an idea which is integral to his theory of the Renaissance and which he sees embodied first in Cimabue. In this connection we should note the specific title of Vasari's work: *Le vite de' più eccellenti pittori, scultori ed architettori*. The words "most excellent" reveal much about Vasari's viewpoint in excluding thirteenth century painting, none of which would merit such praise.

Yet the very degree of his derogation of the art of that remote epoch is a register of its importance in his scheme of things. This is the foil against which he measured almost everything that happened in the *buona maniera moderna* of the Renaissance. For Vasari this periodization was so important that he would not see individuality, let alone anything progressive, in an artist such as Guido da Siena.

If perchance he saw or had heard of the 1221 date inscribed on the Palazzo Pubblico *Madonna,* this would have signified all the more that Guido was part and parcel of the old "Greek" style. If he could have known of our modern disputes over that date and over the place of Guido in the thirteenth century, he would certainly have considered it a matter of no great moment.

If Vasari, thorough as he is, is silent about Guido da Siena, so are the other early Florentine writers. When Ghiberti does no more than cite the name of Cimabue as a sort of agent to get him into his Giotto tale, we can scarcely be surprised at the omission of Guido's name, an artist who would have represented for him nothing but that crudity of the Byzantine style which he so disliked. Yet it is just in this period of the late thirteenth century that some vital steps toward the Renaissance are taken. Unlike Ghiberti and Vasari, we are deeply interested in the very process of transformation from the old manner to the new. Among the important artists in the Tuscany of that time, and one who had his share in shaping the evolution of Italian art, was Guido da Siena.

No existing document or inscription of the thirteenth century mentions the name of Guido da Siena. We know the name only from the inscription on the Palazzo Pubblico *Madonna*; but this inscription is an accretion of the early fourteenth century. Undoubtedly the text for it was taken from the Siena Polyptych No. 7 (Fig. 7), but since that panel has been cut down to exclude the name of Guido, it follows we are dealing with a legend of an artist by that name. Nevertheless, we may give credence to the fourteenth century evidence and assume that the paintings associated in style with the Palazzo Pubblico *Madonna* do represent the oeuvre of an artist named Guido.

This echo of a name does not provide much in the way of biography. None of the references to artists named Guido culled from the archives of the time seem to be identical with our Guido. We have, then, no documents of commission or payment, no tax declarations or lawsuits, and no death notice. But if works of art be acceptable evidence, we know quite a bit about the painter: when he flourished, what sorts of things he painted, the scope of his shop down to the last reverberation of it in the early part of the next century.

Guido emerges as a clearly perceived personality who can charm with his composition and his linear grace. He registers for us the impact of such giants as Coppo di Marcovaldo and Cimabue, and at the same time he himself contributes to the flowering of Tuscan art. The endless disputation over the date at which Guido worked has only obscured our picture of him. Once we assign him a place in the second half of the thirteenth century instead of that remote time around 1221, thus stripping his works of a specious precocity the earlier date imposes, we are in a position to appraise more accurately his intrinsic artistic worth as well as his immense importance as the founder or crystallizer of a Sienese kind of painting.

A search through the Guidesque oeuvre turns up a surprising piece of information about his beginnings. The small Reliquary Shutters (Figs. 1-6, Cat. No. I) with scenes of St. Francis, St. Clare, St. Catherine of Alexandria, and St. Bartholomew, traditionally considered the poorest sort of work from the shop of Guido, reveal on closer study a quality unequaled except in other autograph works by Guido. Unquestionably we have here the earliest preserved work from his hand. The scenes have about them all the earmarks of an artist's juvenilia; the naïve vivacity and density of narrative detail bespeak the zeal of the novice. The stocky, animated robots, the cardboard buildings and the nearly spaceless stages they occupy are characteristic of the period around the middle of the thirteenth century. We can find these features in such works as the Crucifix (Fig. 88) by Coppo di Marcovaldo, the St. Michael Altarpiece in Vico l'Abate near Florence, and in the St. Francis Altarpiece (Fig. 124) in the Bardi Chapel of Santa Croce. From these comparisons as well as from our study of Guido's later works, a date of about 1260 would be likely for the Reliquary Shutters. We may deduce, further, that the painter was probably just emerging as an independent artist when he executed this work. According to traditional estimates in such matters, we might suppose that the artist was around twenty years of age and that he was born, therefore, close to 1240.

These Reliquary Shutters suggest something else of a biographical nature for they contain a distinct flavor or reminiscence of Bonaventura Berlinghieri, the Lucchese painter whose only preserved work is the 1235 St. Francis Altarpiece (Figs. 62-64) in Pescia. One suspects it is he—and not such Florentine masters as Coppo, the St. Michael Master, or the Bardi St. Francis Master—who influenced Guido in his formative stage. Bonaventura and the Sienese artist share a decorative grace and lyrical mood which is never to the same degree found in the Florentine masters. At innumerable points Guido's Reliquary Shutters draw close to the Pescia painting: the buildings and their decorative details, the configurations of the hillocks, the figure style. The flat stage sets behind the figures (which Guido will later abandon) and the entire concept of pictorial space are remarkably similar. Above all, Guido and Bonaventura share a love of flat, dark shapes silhouetted against the gold ground, which gives their works an elegantly austere mood.

Speculating about the early training of Guido da Siena, we may look to Siena itself or turn to Florence or to Lucca. Siena appears to offer little, although this may be due to the fact that so little is known of painting in that city earlier in the thirteenth century and that so few examples are preserved. Florence certainly offered more possibilities but it would have been an alien atmosphere for the artist and, anyway, the correspondences are not striking enough to warrant the idea of an apprenticeship in that city. In favor of a relation between Guido and Lucca is the prominence of that school of painting in the early thirteenth century. Lucchese influence, especially through the Berlinghieri family, is felt all over Tuscany and, as we have recently discovered (Bib. 72), extended by mid century as far as Bologna where a Lucchese, possibly Marco Berlinghieri, painted a fresco cycle. Above all, Bonaventura Berlinghieri, besides being a painter unsurpassed in all Tuscany at that time, was also influential as a teacher. It is quite possible that Guido had a sojourn in Lucca and perhaps a period of training there sometime during the 1250's. The connection with Lucca is often to be seen in Guidesque painting, not only in iconography and composition but also in mood and sentiment.

Other influences come into play in the later works of Guido, the Polyptych No. 7 (Fig. 7), the Lenten Hanging (Fig. 10), both of the 1270's, and the San Domenico Altarpiece of the 1280's, composed of the Palazzo Pubblico *Madonna* (Figs. 14-15) and the Badia Ardenga narratives (Figs. 18, 20-30). Unquestionably the two greatest forces in this later development of Guido's art are Coppo di Marcovaldo and Cimabue, about whom a word may be said here. Coppo di Marcovaldo, one of the great painters and innovators in Florentine art, is still a little-known and shadowy figure.

Nevertheless, the major lines of his artistic personality can be traced. Taken prisoner by the Sienese in the Battle of Montaperti in 1260, he brought Florentine art to Siena with his *Madonna* (Fig. 80), signed and dated 1261, which was painted for the Servi Church of Siena. To him is also attributed the large *Madonna* (Fig. 81) in the Servi Church of Orvieto, probably of the late 1260's, as well as the Crucifix (Fig. 88) in San Gimignano of the 1250's. His *Madonnas*, besides being painted in an unprecedentedly monumental scale, speak a whole new language of forms and sentiments, all of which must have deeply impressed Guido. Banished from Coppo's work was much of the iconic quality of the figures, that frontality of the Virgin, the paper-thin throne, all of which Guido had been accustomed to in such works as the *Madonna* (Fig. 79), then probably in the Cathedral and now in the Opera del Duomo of Siena. The new humanity and, at the same time, the enhanced majesty of the Virgin, her dynamic posture, the placing of the Child at arm's length as though he really were a child and not a symbol, the plastic quality of the throne on which she sits, the sense of measurable space around the figures—all these things must have left Guido wonderstruck.

Nevertheless, there is evidence, even in Guido's earlier Madonnas, that the style of Coppo held second place to that of Cimabue. Cimabue, a younger Florentine, must have emerged as a major figure in the 1260's. Documents indicate he was already an important personage by the early 1270's. It is here, we believe, that one should place his program of frescoes in the choir and transepts of the upper church of St. Francis at Assisi. The *Madonna with St. Francis* (Fig. 72) in the lower church at Assisi, more evolved in spatial concepts than the scenes in the upper church, probably belongs to a slightly later point, but before 1280. The climax of his career would appear to be the Trinita *Madonna* (Fig. 126), datable in the 1290's, which, in many ways, sums up the achievements of Dugento Tuscan artists, but which was too late to affect Guido.

Inevitably Guido turned to Cimabue, who certainly was one of the supreme geniuses of Italian art and who consummately expresses all the major creative aims of Tuscan painting. More vigorously than most artists then or later, Cimabue struggled to define plastic masses set into measurable volumes and to express human relationships and emotions. It is indeed unimaginable that the Sienese artist would not have been profoundly influenced by his Florentine contemporary. Cimabue's influence on Guido took shape in a number of ways, one of which was the new comprehension of mass and volume in paintings of the Madonna Enthroned. Four *Madonnas* from the shop and following of Cimabue, variously dated, apparently reflect an early formula Cimabue devised for the representation of the Madonna Enthroned. These are the *Madonnas* in the Acton Collection, Florence (Fig. 96), in San Remigio, Florence (Fig. 97), in the Galleria Sabauda, Turin (Fig. 98), and in Sant' Andrea, Mosciano (Fig. 99). All of these probably have as a prototype one by Cimabue himself in which the cubic density of the boxlike throne on which the Madonna sits would have been emphasized by the diagonal recession of one of the sides. This is certainly a step beyond Coppo with his limited suggestions of three-dimensional mass. It seems unlikely that this stage was reached before the 1270's; it is equally certain that Cimabue, and not Coppo or Guido, evolved this vigorous new statement. In Cimabue's own work this stage is seen in the fresco of the Virgin in Glory (Fig. 95) in the upper church at Assisi where the complex throne and its tiered footstool are given dimensionality by the diagonal views. Since all the Guidesque representations of the Madonna Enthroned have such thrones with a deep recession along one side, including, unquestionably, the now mutilated *Madonna* (Fig. 3) from San Bernardino, it seems clear that they all have as a premise the formula of the inventive Cimabue. There is little doubt that Coppo's visual world was outdated by about 1270 and that the new artistic force was Cimabue.

Cimabue exerted enormous influence in the solution of spatial problems, the most important task the Dugento artists set themselves. The throne was, of course, only one of the objects used to generate a third dimension. Cimabue also created a depth in his pictures by the use of elaborate architectural settings. Thus, the astonishing fresco of the Fall of Babel in the upper church at Assisi plunges us into a variety of spatial experiences unprecedented in Western art since Pompeian Fourth Style extravagances. It is in this light that we should view the tilted planes and recessions of the architectural stage sets of Guido's mature narrative paintings, the scenes from the Badia Ardenga (Figs. 18, 20-30).

Insofar as Cimabue by the sheer power of his imagery set his stamp on the age, Guido may be seen to have appropriated not only a whole kit of technical details but something of the new animus as well. An example of this is Guido's scene of the *Crucifixion* (Fig. 28). The similarity to the *Crucifixion* (Fig. 89) in the upper church at Assisi by Cimabue leaves little doubt that Guido knew it. All the compositional devices are the same, though necessarily simplified in the small panel by Guido. But while a comparison of such elements as composition and gestures is instructive and convincing, the relationship goes deeper. In both scenes the emotional response of the figures inspires compassion in the spectator. Cimabue, and Guido after him, translate the drama into a very immediate and human experience. This cannot be said of Duccio's ethereal, extramundane interpretation in his *Maestà* or Giotto's intellectual and introspective *Crucifixion* in the Arena Chapel. It is significant that in another scene, the *Assumption* in the upper church at Assisi, Cimabue presents the Virgin as swooning; thus he conveys the emotion of a figure undergoing, simultaneously, dizzying physical ascent and exaltation. And Guido, in his *Mounting of the Cross* (Fig. 26), subjects us to a comparable emotion as the Virgin passionately tries to restrain Christ from climbing the ladder to the cross.

All these are fundamental changes in the pictorial concepts of the thirteenth century. Certainly these new concepts originated with Coppo di Marcovaldo and Cimabue. Despite this it would be unfair to consider Guido as little more than an imitator; he borrowed as any artist would in any age. That Guido absorbed these fundamental changes so completely is already praise enough. That he incorporated them into a Sienese scheme of painting is a matter of more historic importance. Guido's works declare their Sienese origin at every turn and, in fact, much of what we mean when we say "Sienese" took root in his paintings. Nowhere in Cimabue or indeed in Coppo can be found that sense of refinement and delicacy which permeates even the gigantic figure of the Palazzo Pubblico *Madonna*; nowhere that sense for silhouette and swift-running contour, that delight in pattern. In many ways Guido is diametrically opposed to the artistic aims of the Florentines. Where they declare ponderous masses and probe into the depth of the picture space, Guido, even using their compositional devices, turns all to decorative account. Where their figures are solemn, his cannot hide a certain charm. Where they try to impress, he beguiles. Where, to take a technical point, Cimabue tools his gold background in a perfunctory and often even unrefined manner, Guido spins elaborately delicate patterns over the gold ground. Much of this, as we know, springs from the temper of the Sienese. Much of it, too, reflects the artistic nature of Guido. But whether it is Sienese or Guidesque, the fact remains that such artists as Duccio, Simone Martini, and even an artist as late as Sassetta in the fifteenth century, are the artistic and spiritual heirs of Guido da Siena.

Even a cursory glance at Guido's oeuvre establishes the fact that he produced two kinds of paintings: what we may call monumental works and, on the other hand, small, narrative scenes. The artistic problems involved differ accordingly.

The earliest preserved monumental work by Guido is the Polyptych (Fig. 7) which Guido painted in the early 1270's. It originally consisted of a Madonna flanked by three saints on either side (Fig. 9a) but it was subsequently cut down by one figure on each end. The spacious setting and the monumental figures are unsurpassed in any comparable dossal with half-length figures of the thirteenth century, as we can see, for example, by comparing it to Meliore's 1271 Polyptych (Fig. 74) in the Uffizi. The importance of Guido's painting is enhanced by the fact it contains the only preserved large-scale heads by his own hand. Here we can see the master in what may be called his middle period when his personal style was well-formulated. The picture has an important place in Sienese and, therefore, in Italian painting. For the first time we see those elaborate and artful patterns of draperies and shapes, and those elegant stuffs which are always to be so noteworthy in Sienese painting. Especially in the faces of the Virgin and the Magdalen, but also in the Evangelist, there is something of that charm which illumines all Sienese painting. When we speculate on the original appearance of the Madonna of the Palazzo Pubblico panel of about a decade later, we would do well to gaze at her earlier counterpart in the Polyptych No. 7.

One of the most important categories of works produced in Guido's shop are the monumental Madonnas Enthroned. It is probable that Guido did not create his first large-scale Madonna until around 1270, some years after Coppo's 1261 *Madonna*. That Guido was influenced by Coppo is shown not only by the comparable large scale of his Madonnas but also by such details as the throneback and the Virgin's white veil (Figs. 31, 32). Yet the rectangular panel shape found in the *Madonnas* of Coppo (Figs. 80, 81) seems to have gone out of fashion. When we observe that even in the later of these paintings, the *Madonna* in Orvieto, Coppo had barely eked out an adequate space above the Virgin's head, we realize that the gabled form is at least later than Coppo. The shape is, in fact, ubiquitous in the last decades of the thirteenth century. It appears in every one of the Enthroned Madonna panels which came from Guido's shop, including the Palazzo Pubblico *Madonna* which must be visualized with its accompanying pediment piece. Furthermore, both the San Bernardino and Arezzo panels (Figs. 31, 32) originally terminated in a simple gable, in both cases cut down to an arched shape at later dates. It is interesting to discover that the gable is not used in those four Cimabuesque *Madonnas* (Figs. 96-99) mentioned above which reflect the early period of Cimabue and which are cast in the old rectangular format used by Coppo. The first instance of a gabled panel in the Cimabuesque oeuvre is that in the Servi Church of Bologna (*Giottesca*, fig. 84a). But this work, while filled with such archaisms as the Coppesque half-length angels behind the throneback, also shows unmistakable repercussions of Duccio's Rucellai *Madonna* (Fig. 125) in that very particular silhouetting of the chair-throne and the stepped footstool against the gold ground. It is patently a work of the late 1280's. The absence of the gable shape from the group of earlier Cimabuesque *Madonnas* is evidence that the form probably originated with Guido, whence it went to Duccio and then, through his Rucellai *Madonna*, to the Florentine school.

In the Palazzo Pubblico *Madonna* (Figs. 14, 15) Guido inserts a cusped, molded arch over the head of the Virgin with triads of angels in the spandrels above. This new fashion is essentially Gothic and ultimately derives from the North. The cusped arch appears first in Guido's early Reliquary Shutters where it serves as an architectural frame for the figures. Guido then adapted this motif for the Madonna in his Polyptych No. 7 and, still later, for his Palazzo Pubblico *Madonna*. The form does not, of course, appear in Coppo's Madonnas, nor do we find it in the Madonnas by Cimabue and his following, although Cimabue does employ the cusped arch in several ways in the upper church of St. Francis in Assisi: in his scene of the Death of the Virgin where a painted cusped arch circumscribes the scene, and in the transept where Cimabuesque angels peer out from behind arcades of cusped arches (Fig. 77). It is Guido who adapted it to the Madonna Enthroned representation. Duccio rejects it in favor of the round arch but the form, somewhat altered, returns with Simone Martini (Fig. 78) and is, of course, stock-in-trade throughout the fourteenth century. We have good evidence, therefore, that Guido made several important innovations in the Madonna format, the use of the gable shape as well as the graceful cusped arch: proof, if proof be needed, of his independence and originality.

Not all Guidesque paintings of the Madonna Enthroned follow the same pattern. At a certain point, in fact, Guido changed the formula in a number of ways and an examination of the differences throws considerable light on his development. Basically there are two groups. The San Bernardino and Arezzo *Madonnas* belong to the earlier group as does the Florence *Madonna,* even though it has some late features. The Galli-Dunn and San Gimignano *Madonnas* group around the Palazzo Pubblico *Madonna* and constitute a later type. The Montaione *Madonna* and the Madonna in the Krakow Tabernacle, on the other hand, are at a certain remove from the strict shop formulas.

The San Bernardino and Arezzo *Madonnas* (Figs. 31, 32) are so close in both general and specific ways that the latter must be accounted a copy of the former, except, of course, in the omission of the medallions. If this is so, good evidence is supplied for the belief that the San Bernardino *Madonna* was originally, like the one in Arezzo, a full-length Madonna seated on a throne of which one side was visible. The throne style of the Arezzo panel follows that established by Cimabue in his early phase, not only in the use of the diagonal side but in the general blockiness of the over-all shape and in the type of ornamentation in rows of large, leafy patterns. But if these two panels are at once later than Coppo and yet done with a cognizance of Cimabue's formula, there are, nevertheless, a number of features which still place them early in Guido's oeuvre. In both panels the Child sits bolt upright, as he does in the Guidesque polyptychs datable in the 1270's and very much as he had in Coppo's Siena panel of 1261. Furthermore, in the Arezzo and San Bernardino *Madonnas* the Virgin grips a fold of the maphorium underneath the Child, as she does also in the *Madonna* in Florence, whereas a new solution is found in the later grouping. The white headcloth of the Virgin falls in gentle waves around the head, ending in a sharp point on the Virgin's breast. This is the way Coppo had arranged it in his Siena *Madonna.* While it recurs in the Krakow Tabernacle and the San Gimignano *Madonna,* it is by then an archaism. Obviously the example of Coppo is still important in such matters even though the newer influence of Cimabue has intervened in other respects. All things considered, it would seem that the Arezzo and San Bernardino *Madonnas* represent the type of the Enthroned Madonna in Guido's shop in the 1270's.

In the later group, of which the Palazzo Pubblico *Madonna* (Fig. 14) is the key work, significant differences are discovered. The Child now leans back with his legs crossed and gazes up at his mother, small effects which nevertheless go far toward establishing a human relationship between these two figures. In these later panels the maphorium falls in a sickle shape beneath the Child's body while the Virgin now supports him with her left hand. The Florence *Madonna* (Fig. 39) betrays its lateness in the sickle-shaped maphorium, one bit of which, however, the Virgin still clasps in her hand. The change in the headcloth in this group consists chiefly in the addition of those gold striations which Guido had already used in the headcloth in his earlier Polyptych. Not until the Montaione *Madonna* (Fig. 54) does the Guido shop succumb to the Cimabuesque style and abandon the white headcloth altogether.

It is only in the group of later Madonnas that we find the cusped arch discussed earlier; it is so deft a termination and delineation of the space around and above the Virgin's head that we are not surprised to find it present in every one of the later panels, even though, in the quite late San Gimignano version (Fig. 60) it is reduced to a painted band rather than a relief molding. In the later type of Guidesque Enthroned Madonna the forward side of the throne has a lathed finial on each corner, establishing a forward plane behind which the throne and the figures recede. This space marker does not appear in the four early Cimabuesque *Madonnas* cited above nor in the Arezzo and San Bernardino *Madonnas*. Its genesis is to be found, once again, in a type which Cimabue must have introduced: the carpentered, wood-lathed chair-throne used in the fresco of the *Madonna with St. Francis* (Fig. 72) in the lower church at Assisi as well as the Cimabuesque *Madonna* in the Servi Church, Bologna. Apparently, then, an old Byzantine formula introduced into Tuscan painting by Cimabue in the 1270's was absorbed in the Guido shop by about 1280.

But of course more than a finial separates the two categories of Guidesque Madonnas. The throne of the Arezzo panel (Fig. 32) and, presumably, that of the San Bernardino *Madonna*, was an unbroken block whereas in the later examples there tend to be fenestrations such as the diminutive arcades in the thrones of the Galli-Dunn and Florence panels (Figs. 43, 39), as well as the throne in the St. Peter Altarpiece (Fig. 54), and probably in the original design of the throne in the Palazzo Pubblico *Madonna* (Fig. 73). That they no longer appear on the throne of the San Gimignano *Madonna* (Fig. 60) indicates the lateness of that variant, painted when the new, Ducciesque marble inlay had come into fashion. Such perforations in the mass of the throne must reflect that chair style introduced by Cimabue. In the category of later Guidesque Madonnas, the seat of the throne recedes at right angles to the picture plane; this more sophisticated comprehension of visual phenomena, undoubtedly due to the researches of Cimabue, is immediately perceived in the Palazzo Pubblico *Madonna*. The painter of the Galli-Dunn *Madonna* had trouble absorbing this idea but the painter of the Florence panel, although he clings to certain features of the earlier Madonna formula, manages very well with the recession of the seat of the throne, as he does also with the placement of the finials.

A recital of such details is profitable. We discover two distinct formulas for Guidesque Madonnas, yielding a chronology and providing rather conclusive evidence for the dating of Guido's monumental works. We also discover the nature of his borrowings from other artists and the fact that Cimabue influenced him in several successive phases. Furthermore, some measure of Guido's originality can be taken. Above all, it helps us to appreciate his achievement in the Palazzo Pubblico *Madonna*. By contrast, other Guidesque Madonnas seem constrained to a very limited space. It is interesting to see the dimensions of the Palazzo Pubblico panel juxtaposed with those of other large Madonnas from the latter part of the thirteenth century and to realize how, in this too, the *Madonna* fits into the tendencies of that time. The wide swinging arc of the throneback, the expanse of gold ground, the breadth of the throne and the sideways posture of the Virgin all emphasize the large, generous space. The tightly packed area above in the spandrels serves to amplify the space below. Not a jot of this was understood by the painter of the Galli-Dunn *Madonna,* who was involved with imitation and reduction of a prototype. The painter of the San Gimignano *Madonna* comprehended better. But the one who really profited was Duccio as may be observed in the clusters of enraptured angels around the Madonna in his *Maestà,* a motif which had its auspicious debut in the spandrels of Guido's Palazzo Pubblico *Madonna* and which then became a part of the Sienese mode. But more important than the borrowing of various motifs, was the understanding Duccio must have gotten about figures and spaces, as may be realized by an analysis of his large, grand Rucellai *Madonna* (Fig. 125) of 1285. Here is where it becomes clear that Guido and Duccio are of successive generations.

A good deal of Guido's time as well as that of his assistants must have gone into the designing and painting of monumental figures, such as the Madonnas Enthroned just discussed. Nevertheless, it is with the smaller paintings that he expresses his artistic personality most fully. The narratives have more spontaneity, more drama, more felicity in composition, and it is in the light of these qualities that they should be examined.

The early style is revealed in those diminutive melodramas on the Reliquary Shutters (Figs. 1-6), which we have already dated about 1260. They are conceived in a Romanesque manner, that is, with forms set on a narrow stage against a flat backdrop and with tightly painted, square-headed figures posed mechanically. Danger, agony, and bloodshed are Guido's ingredients here. Even in the *Stigmatization of St. Francis* the religious ecstasy has a certain naïvely vigorous quality about it. In all four scenes the staccato rhythms of figures and compositions are very different from the sonorous measures Guido achieved in his later narratives.

The difference is already apparent in the Lenten Hanging (Figs. 10-13) Guido painted in the early 1270's. In the interval between the Reliquary Shutters and these three narratives the potent influence of Cimabue intervenes. In a larger sense, though, it is not so much Cimabue as it is a forceful influx at a certain point in the thirteenth century of Byzantinism, of which Cimabue is the leading exponent. In the Lenten Hanging this Byzantinism is observed first of all in the figures, especially in the representations of Christ. Taller, more slender, endowed with softer features, with more grace of movement, the figures have lost the puppet-like quality observed in the Reliquary Shutters. The scenes of the Lenten Hanging also mark a fundamental turning-point spatially. In the *Raising of Lazarus* we can see the receding diagonal of the side of the building in the rear. This should be related to the development of the three-dimensional properties taking place at about the same time in the monumental paintings, specifically the throne as we believe it was in the San Bernardino *Madonna*.

The three narratives of the Lenten Hanging have a poetic quality unequaled in Guido's oeuvre. In the *Transfiguration* a luminescent atmosphere spreads over the entire surface; the formations of the rocks and the patterns of the draperies constitute one of the high points of Dugento painting. The supernal mood depends directly on these abstractions of rock and drapery and on these rigidly traditional poses. On the other hand, in the *Entry into Jerusalem* Guido treats such traditional elements as the boys perched in the trees or those throwing cloaks before the ass with an exuberance that exceeds even Duccio's. And he is Duccio's match when it comes to anecdotal detail: the woman who holds up her infant to Christ, or the man with the two small boys looking back toward Christ, one clasping his father's hand and the other perched on his shoulder. The delight in almost garrulous narrative is seen to be already a fact of Sienese painting a generation earlier than its most celebrated exponent.

The twelve narratives from the Badia Ardenga (Figs. 18, 20-30), originally part of the San Domenico Altarpiece, are clearly works of Guido's maturity. Here, more fluent figures inhabit spaces measured by stage properties of great plastic definition. At the same time every scene is reduced to the simplest terms so that individually and together they maintain the necessary visual coherence in the larger context of the great Altarpiece. In the tradition of Byzantine mosaics and manuscript illuminations, figures are silhouetted against a gold ground. Architectural elements serve chiefly as foils to the figures (the Virgin's tower in the *Annunciation*) or as spatial repoussoirs (the lateral buildings in the *Crucifixion*). It is typical of Guido that the baldacchino in the *Presentation of Christ in the Temple* is related decoratively but not physically to the figures. While his staging devices are of the simplest, Guido nevertheless achieves some remarkable effects as, for instance, in the *Flight into Egypt* where a somber and brooding landscape heightens the mysteriousness and secrecy of the flight and, uncannily, suggests the cover of night. Throughout the series Guido maintains this dramatic level, as in such simple and intensely spiritual tableaux as the *Crucifixion* and the *Flagellation*.

Guido's relation to the next generation can be gauged in such a scene as the *Nativity*. It is cast in the familiar Byzantine format including the cave, the elliptical couch of the Virgin, the first bath of Christ, the attendant angels and shepherds, and the figure of Joseph. The isolated Virgin broods, out of time and space, on the destiny of Christ. How different Giotto will be in his Padua *Nativity* where human actions and emotions are decisive: it is significant that Giotto shows the poignant moment when the Virgin surrenders the Child to a nursemaid. Guido's narratives helped prepare the way for the next generation of Giotto and Duccio; the enormous differences between the early Reliquary Shutters and the late Badia Ardenga scenes make this clear.

Guido is, in many ways, the founding father of Sienese narrative painting. This genre is comprised on the one hand of spatial complexity and dynamic narrative situation, and in this aspect its followers will be Duccio, the Lorenzetti, and such a later artist as Domenico di Bartolo. On the other hand, Sienese narrative is also a decorative, abstract, and lyrical kind of painting. In this Guido has great issue. His noblest and closest heir will be Simone Martini, the essence of whose genius may be said to lie just in the fact that he comprehended so well the juxtaposition of those superb shapes silhouetted against the gold and in tense relation to one another. Closely akin are Guido's *Annunciation* in Princeton and Simone's *Annunciation* in the Uffizi. In Guido da Siena all the flavor and poetry of Sienese art are already apparent.

The foregoing discussion has dealt primarily with Guido's own work since this forms the basis for our understanding of the nature of Guidesque painting in general. However, since relatively little has survived, our conception of Guido may be extended by an examination of the shop work. This is true because it is to be assumed that Guido had a large share in the underlying concept of many of these paintings and because certain works may reflect lost prototypes by the master. It is possible to distinguish a number of hands and to trace the development of the entire Guidesque oeuvre, decade by decade, from the 1260's into the beginning of the fourteenth century.

A brief sketch of this development, which registers the rise and decline of the shop, begins with Guido's early Reliquary Shutters (Figs. 1-6). Besides the Shutters, we cannot point to a single other painting which was done during the decade of the 1260's. Attributions of other Guidesque works to this period are not, as we shall see, defensible. It must, though, have been a time of great change with some considerable new influences shaping Guido's art.

The two works which Guido himself painted in the early part of the 1270's, the Siena Polyptych No. 7 (Fig. 7) and the Lenten Hanging (Fig. 10), give an image of an artist far more assured than he was when he painted the Shutters. None of the other works datable in the decade of the 1270's can by any stretch of the critical faculties be attributed to Guido himself. There is little doubt that by this time we are confronted with a workshop situation. Probably Guido worked alone without assistance in the 1260's, as indeed any youthful artist would do, but impelled by the volume of work he must by the time of the 1270's have taken on a number of assistants. Most of the paintings datable to this period reveal a variety of hands and, in fact, specific assistants can be identified, most of whom are to reappear later on. Despite the variety, all these works betray such a coherence of style and fidelity to the Guidesque formula that we must assume a closely knit workshop arrangement under the direct tutelage of the master, Guido.

The Polyptych No. 6 in the Siena Academy (Fig. 33), a less than inspired variant of Guido's own Polyptych, must be placed in this period, introducing us to an assist-

14

ant who follows Guido's formulas more scrupulously than most and whom we call the Madonna del Voto Master on the basis of his masterpiece. We must also place in this decade the Reliquary Shutters depicting scenes from the life of Beato Gallerani (Figs. 35, 36), a work which can be associated with the Master of the St. Peter Altarpiece. The painter of the San Bernardino *Madonna* (Fig. 31) also appears, as does the weaker assistant responsible for the copy of that work, the Arezzo *Madonna* (Fig. 32). The painting of the *Lord and Virgin Enthroned* (Fig. 34) also dates from the 1270's, so that still another reputable lieutenant, the so-called Clarisse Master, was on the scene at that time. From extant paintings alone, therefore, we can identify five assistants in the bottega in the 1270's.

In the 1280's significant changes took place. The inevitable multiplication of tasks, requiring a further expansion of the bottega, must have kept Guido even busier in a supervisory capacity though, as we shall see, a greater latitude was given to the individual painters. And, as we believe to have been the case, one of them was entrusted with the execution of the important commission for a new altarpiece for the Siena Cathedral. Guido himself must have been heavily occupied with the monumental Altarpiece for San Domenico, the central panel of which is the *Madonna* in the Palazzo Pubblico. The magnitude of that altarpiece and its probable situation on the high altar of the vast, new, and important church of San Domenico tell us much about Guido's status in his native city of Siena in the early 1280's.

Since no work bearing Guido's personal touch can be found after the first part of the 1280's, we may believe either that he died in that decade or stopped painting. Whatever the truth may be, it is clear that the shop continued to be vital throughout the period. The radical change in its output is due partly to the increased number of assistants with the consequent dilution of the Guidesque formula.

Most of the assistants who were there in the seventies continue to produce paintings. The personality in the shop who undergoes the least metamorphosis is the Madonna del Voto Master, the painter of the Polyptych No. 6. He is still the most faithful follower of Guido's formulas. His *Madonna del Voto* (Fig. 37) and, probably, the Florence *Madonna* (Fig. 39) register only the major changes of the time, while his painting technique shows no relaxation with the passing of time. He is not a vibrant personality by any means, though his very docility may have been pleasing to Guido.

The St. Peter Master continues in the shop with his *Last Judgment* from Grosseto (Fig. 49) and, late in the decade or in the 1290's, his greatest work, the St. Peter Altarpiece (Fig. 53). In this work, however, he begins to assert an independence of style or, rather, to fall under the newer influence of Duccio. This independence is also seen in one more work which may be attributed to his hand, the Montaione *Madonna* (Fig. 54), also of the late 1280's or thereafter.

The Clarisse Master, too, shows an evolution away from Guido, although his work suffers from the divergence, as can be seen in the Polyptych he executed during the

1280's (Fig. 50). The continued presence of the San Bernardino Master is verified by the Princeton *Madonna* (Fig. 42), where a tendency toward a softening of the earlier formula is also to be detected.

We can identify four important new hands in the work of the period although if all Guidesque paintings were preserved, we might find that they had been active in the shop earlier. Thus the painter of the Galli-Dunn *Madonna* (Fig. 43) was probably no newcomer to the shop, even though there is no certain trace of his hand before the 1280's. As it is, we know him only from this variant on the Palazzo Pubblico *Madonna*. Nor can we find earlier traces of the painter of the Courtauld *Coronation of the Virgin* (Fig. 44) although this capable assistant gives every indication of being an old hand with Guidesque formulas, and in this work may have been following a design by Guido himself. The palimpsest of *St. Dominic* in the Fogg Museum (Fig. 48) appears to be by still another hand working in the shop during the 1280's. On the other hand, the painter of the Crucifixion panel at Yale University (Fig. 52) seems to have a quite tenuous connection with the shop, perhaps having helped out with lesser parts of the Badia Ardenga narratives.

Although fundamental differences occurred in the workshop in the 1280's, certainly by the 1290's everything had changed. Was Guido no longer on the scene? Did the onslaught of Duccio's *stil nuovo* bring about a dissolution of Guido's workshop and the decline of an outmoded style? In any case the evidence is clear. The first sign of it is probably contained in the St. Peter Altarpiece (Fig. 53), which in its light tonalities and softly painted forms may possibly not even have been painted in the shop of Guido.

This sort of independence is, in general, characteristic of all the works produced in the 1290's. The Clarisse Master shows his emancipation and his susceptibility to newer influences in the two works datable in the 1290's, the Krakow Tabernacle (Figs. 56-58) and the Cross in San Gimignano (Fig. 55). In certain features of these works we sense the absence of Guido or, rather, the degree to which the painter has removed himself from Guido.

The Wellesley Tabernacle center (Fig. 59), cast in a format of the 1280's, is so provincial in style as to suggest that the painter may have executed it later. If he had been in the shop for a sojourn, he may have picked up enough of the formulas to paint this marginally Guidesque work. We may also place in the 1290's or later the San Gimignano *Madonna* (Fig. 60) since its simplification of a Guidesque original (the Palazzo Pubblico *Madonna*) is so drastic and the Ducciesque influences so pronounced. We may speak of the artist as a follower of Guido rather than an assistant, though he must have had training in the shop. In any case the thread between this work and the work it imitates, between this artist and Guido, has become extremely tenuous.

Finally, there is but a remote echo of the once bustling shop and of Guido's art in the St. Francis Altarpiece (Fig. 61), which in its careful assimilation of the St.

Francis legend from the fresco cycle of the upper church of St. Francis at Assisi betrays its lateness. That it can be robed in the long-discarded garments of Guidesque style reveals a tenacious follower of Guido or the taste of a patron who, at this incredibly late date, still esteems the *maniera greca.*

A chronological graph of extant Guidesque works would show a surprising rise from the single painting by Guido himself in the 1260's to the seven items of the 1270's, including two by Guido, to the twelve in the next decade, including Guido's San Domenico Altarpiece. Thereafter such a graph would show a sharp decline to four works in the 1290's, none of which are by Guido himself, and to one work toward the end of the first decade of the fourteenth century, long after Guido must have left the scene.

Even without the proof of document or literary reference to tell us so, we sense a cloud over Guido's later career. During the 1280's it is the story of the master's decreasing hold on his assistants who fell increasingly under newer influences. Certainly Duccio had swept the field from Guido by mid decade, at the time when Duccio was called to the city of Florence to paint the Rucellai *Madonna.* We are justified in believing that Guido and his shop went into a swift decline by the end of the decade. In all this there is a curious parallel to the story Dante tells:

> Credette Cimabue nella pittura
> Tener lo campo, ed ora ha Giotto il grido
> > *(Purgatorio,* XI, 94)

A decade or so earlier the very same thing had transpired in the city of Siena when the light from Duccio's new art effectively extinguished that of Guido's.

> Sì che la fama di colui è oscura.

CATALOGUE

Notes for the Use of the Catalogue

The first four entries of the Catalogue deal with paintings that are here considered autograph works by Guido. The remaining twenty-one entries cover those paintings that are considered to be by Guido's shop and following. They are arranged chronologically, decade by decade, although their ordering is in some cases not inalterable.

There has been no attempt to group paintings by specific hands since these works are chiefly important as manifestations of the Guidesque style and the greater consideration has been the evolution of the total Guidesque oeuvre. However, other works with which a painting is associated in the oeuvre of a particular hand are signaled in the individual catalogue entry.

An attempt has been made to keep a fairly regular outline in each catalogue entry; the various aspects of each painting are discussed in the following order: condition, provenance, iconographic problems, style, attribution, and dating.

Each catalogue entry is followed by a chronological listing of the bibliography relevant to the particular painting. Here, as well as within the catalogue text itself, bibliographical references are indicated by assigned numbers which refer to the complete bibliography at the end of the book. This bibliography is arranged alphabetically by author.

Because of the frequent reference to three works, the following abbreviations are used throughout instead of bibliography numbers:

Garrison Bib. 73, E. B. Garrison, *Italian Romanesque Panel Painting.*

Marle Bib. 107, R. van Marle, *The Development of the Italian Schools of Painting.*

Giottesca Bib. 176, Sinibaldi and Brunetti, eds., . . . *Catalogo della mostra giottesca* . . .

AUTOGRAPH WORKS

I. *Reliquary Shutters: Martyrdom of St. Bartholomew, Martyrdom of St. Catherine of Alexandria, Stigmatization of St. Francis, St. Clare Repulsing the Saracens*

FIGURES 1-6   Siena Pinacoteca No. 4   H 121.5 x W 71 cm.

There is a vertical split through the St. Clare and St. Francis scenes. The surfaces are scratched and abraded. The two panels were originally reversed so that the episodes of St. Bartholomew and St. Catherine appeared on the left shutter while the St. Francis and St. Clare scenes appeared on the right (Figs. 1, 2).

These Shutters are mentioned in the catalogue of 1864 when they were No. 16 in the Siena gallery. Their earlier history is unknown.

The scenes are from the hand of Guido.

That these panels were designed as reliquary shutters seems conclusive owing to the fact that they are identical in shape and measurement to the Andrea Gallerani panels (Fig. 35), which unquestionably served as covers of a reliquary box. There can be little doubt that the latter are an imitation of Guido's early work. That being the case, it seems likely the assistant would follow a formula for reliquary shutters and not, say, the wings of a folding tabernacle with central image.

The inclusion of episodes from the lives of St. Clare and of St. Francis suggests a Franciscan origin for the work. If so, the Franciscans who ordered the work were interested in doing honor to St. Bartholomew because when the Shutters are reversed, as they must have been, St. Bartholomew has the place of honor in the upper left (Fig. 2). During the thirteenth century St. Bartholomew was one of the four principal saints of the Siena Cathedral. It is possible the Shutters were intended for the Cathedral although the cult was city-wide and, in fact, there was a church dedicated to him near the Porta Camollia (Gigli, Bib. 80, II, p. 136). In any case, this is the earliest preserved representation of the martyrdom of that saint. It is possible that the Shutters were intended to close over a reliquary box containing some relics of St. Bartholomew.

The episode of St. Clare's expulsion of the Saracens who were besieging the walls of her monastery of San Damiano (Fig. 6) is one of the high points of her legend as it was written by Tomaso da Celano sometime between 1255 and 1261. No earlier representation of the scene is known. The *Martyrdom of St. Catherine* (Fig. 5) is also represented in a Pisan Altarpiece with scenes from her legend of the middle of the century (*Giottesca*, fig. 22a).

Ample precedent existed, of course, for the *Stigmatization of St. Francis* (Fig. 4). The most unusual feature of Guido's scene is the three rays emanating from the seraph's mouth to the head of the Saint. As has been pointed out (Bib. 117, pp. 118-

121), rays are a rarity in thirteenth century representations. The single, wide ray from the seraph to the head of the Saint in Bonaventura Berlinghieri's scene in the Pescia Altarpiece of St. Francis (Fig. 62) of 1235 is echoed only in the scene from an Altarpiece by the Magdalen Master of the 1270's in a London collection (Bib. 44, fig. 14). Much closer to the Guidesque scheme are two Florentine representations, both from the mid century, the scene on the St. Francis Altarpiece in Santa Croce, Florence (Fig. 124), and a similar one in the Uffizi (*Giottesca*, fig. 6) in which three rays issue from the seraph to the Saint's halo. The similar arrangement in Guido's scene would suggest a date close in time to these mid-century works. Aside from these examples, rays are not found again in the Stigmatization until their very different appearance in the early fourteenth century. It is interesting that the two later Guidesque versions—that in the Gallerani Shutters (Fig. 100) and that in the St. Francis Altarpiece (Fig. 61)—omit the rays, thus following the more conventional thirteenth century arrangement.

On the other hand, these latter two versions retain the most singular element of Guido's scene, the bears clambering over the rocks and in the trees, a motif never otherwise found in representations of the Stigmatization. Possibly they are to confirm the remote and mountainous site of the Stigmatization; according to St. Bonaventure (Bib. 19, pp. 542-45), it took place "in locum excelsum seorsum qui dicitur mons Alvernae." Possibly, too, they are to be thought of as exemplifying a susceptibility to the charm which the Saint exerted over all of God's creatures. In any case, no textual source has been found to explain the motif.

These narratives have always been relegated to the following of Guido, being considered either inferior to those of the similar Shutters No. 5 in the Siena Pinacoteca (Figs. 35, 36), or else by the same inferior hand which painted them. There can be little doubt, however, that the No. 4 Shutters represent Guido himself at an early point in his career, whereas the No. 5 Shutters, as will be seen, are of lesser quality and by the hand of an assistant at a later time.

The landscape elements can be compared with those in other works which we attribute to the master himself. The *Stigmatization* has elaborately crevassed rocks, sharply articulated with white lines in a technique indistinguishable from that used in the later *Entry into Jerusalem* (Fig. 12) or in the still later *Nativity* (Fig. 20). The leafy plants lend a festive air just as they do in his *Entry into Jerusalem*.

The four scenes have an abundance of architectural elements drawn in an over-meticulous but charming fashion. The inventiveness of these is seen in such things as the tiled roofs, the gleam of light on the cylindrical towers, and the complex patterns of buildings intended as scenic backdrops. These characteristics are to reappear in his other works, especially the *Entry into Jerusalem* (Fig. 12) and the *Raising of Lazarus* (Fig. 13) in the Lenten Hanging, and in a number of scenes from the Badia Ardenga (Figs. 18, 21, 27). As with the landscapes, the architectural elements here are of the same type and of the same caliber as those in Guido's other works.

The figures in all the scenes are conceived with energy and vivacity, not least among them being the tumbling Saracens of the St. Clare episode. The most striking figure, though, is that of St. Francis in the *Stigmatization*. The artist essays a difficult posture with the lower part of the body and the head in profile and the shoulders turned away from the spectator. Although not completely natural, the inventiveness of the posture is commendable.

If there is strong evidence that Guido himself painted these figures, there is as much to indicate that he did so at a point much earlier than the other works attributed to him. The figures, both in draperies and flesh parts, are tightly drawn, with hard and enameled surfaces. The draperies have none of the complex rhythms they will take on later under new Byzantine influences. The faces, in particular those of St. Catherine and the flayers of St. Bartholomew, are square-headed, youthful types and more Romanesque than Guido's later faces, where a more richly modeled Byzantine type is developed. The same is true of the landscape and architectural elements; they have little of that three-dimensionality and simplicity of presentation which Guido will achieve much later in the Badia Ardenga narratives. All these things suggest the relative youthfulness of the artist. When we compare the Shutters to his other works, we are led to conclude that they must have been done around 1260.

The painting cannot have been executed before 1255, the year in which St. Clare was canonized; nor can it be very much later than 1260 as we have seen from the stylistic analysis. Unquestionably it is the earliest painting we have from Guido and from the Guidesque ambient. As such, it should illuminate his early years and artistic background. In contrast to the Badia Ardenga scenes and even the scenes in the Lenten Hanging, the scenes from the Shutters patently belong to an earlier phase of the Dugento, one in which Bonaventura Berlinghieri is a prominent and influential figure. This Lucchese painter is mentioned in documents from 1228 to 1274 (Bib. 75). The similarities are at their strongest in a comparison between the No. 4 Shutters and Bonaventura's *St. Francis* (Fig. 62) of 1235. The treatment of architectural and landscape elements is very close, as are the stocky, gesticulating figures. Guido's mannerisms of style, particularly the schematizations of the faces, vary from the Bonaventuran formula, so that we may hesitate to speak of a workshop arrangement. Nevertheless, it is clear that Bonaventura exerted an enormous influence upon him. One way or another, stylistically and iconographically, traces of a Lucchese and Bonaventuran influence lasted throughout Guido's career.

BIBLIOGRAPHY

1842 Siena, Bib. 156, p. 3.
1864 Siena, Bib. 158, p. 9.
1885 Thode, Bib. 178, p. 150.
1890 Thode, Bib. 179, p. 7.
1895 Siena, Bib. 160, p. 4.
1903 Siena, Bib. 161, p. 4.

1907 Venturi, Bib. 188, v, p. 102.
1907 Jacobsen, Bib. 85, p. 10.
1911 Weigelt, Bib. 191, pp. 216-18, 225.
1915 Dami, Bib. 49, pp. 42, 113.
1922 Weigelt, Bib. 192, p. 282.
1923 Marle, Bib. 107, I, p. 372.

1928 Cecchi, Bib. 31, p. 15.
1929 Sandberg-Vavalà, Bib. 149, pp. 808, 827, 870 n. 15.
1930 Weigelt, Bib. 194, p. 2.
1932 Berenson, Bib. 15, p. 269.
1932 Edgell, Bib. 61, p. 34.
1933 Siena, Bib. 164, p. 114.
1939 Bacci, Bib. 7, pp. 28-29.

1949 Garrison, Bib. 73, No. 352.
1951 Meiss, Bib. 118, pp. 119-20.
1951 Brandi, Bib. 23, p. 255.
1952 Kaftal, Bib. 90, pp. 270-78.
1955 Carli, Bib. 28, p. 30.
1956 White, Bib. 197, pp. 344, 347.
1958 Siena, Bib. 165, pp. 15, 17.

II. *Polyptych: Madonna and Child with SS. Francis, John the Baptist, John the Evangelist, Mary Magdalen*

FIGURES 7-9a, 66, 69   Siena Pinacoteca No. 7   H 85 x W 186 cm.

The panel has been cut down on either end, having originally contained three figures on either side of the Madonna as well as additional words in the inscription. There is a horizontal split across the panel at shoulder level. In the 1931 cleaning repaint was removed from the background, and the inner molding and the haloes were retooled. The oval stones of the halo of the Child are missing. The medallions have lost their contents which may have been bust-length angels. The extant figures are in good condition.

The inscription along the lower frame reads:

   . . . X . . . AMENIS · QUE · XTS · LENIS · NULLIS · VELIT · ANGERE · PENIS: ANNO ·
       DN̄I MILLESIMO · DUCENTESIMO · SEPTUAGESIMO . . .

To the left the wording must have included: *me Guido de Senis diebus pinxit*, on the basis of the Palazzo Pubblico *Madonna* inscription which was presumably copied from this (see Cat. No. IV). On the right, the last unit of the decade is missing; the year could have been anywhere between 1270 and 1279. There is also sufficient space for the day and month.

The panel came to the Pinacoteca in 1867 from the Convento di San Francesco in Colle di Val d'Elsa. The painting must have been in Siena itself until at least the early fourteenth century when its inscription was most probably seen and imitated by Duccio's shop in the restoration of the Palazzo Pubblico *Madonna*.

This painting is from the hand of Guido.

The shape of this Polyptych seems to be Guidesque in origin; all the figures are included under one, low-pitched gable and are at once separated and united by the arcade above their heads (Fig. 9a). The Madonna is placed within a cusped arch, preceding its use in the Palazzo Pubblico *Madonna* (Fig. 14) by a number of years. Polyptychs with half-length figures are to be found in other shapes in contemporary painting, such as Meliore's 1271 Polyptych in the Uffizi (Fig. 74) in which the rectangular format is broken by a projecting gable over the central figure. Of a different type is the Polyptych by Vigoroso da Siena dated 128 . . . (Fig. 75) with its multiple gable scheme. The Ducciesque type would seem to grow out of Vigoroso's, as, for instance, in the Polyptychs Nos. 47 and 28 in the Siena Pinacoteca (Marle, II, figs. 40, 41). Only Deodato Orlandi in his 1301 Polyptych (Fig. 76) in the Museo Civico, Pisa, is seen to be still reliant on Guido.

It is interesting that such a large percentage of the preserved polyptychs bear inscriptions with the name of the artist and the date. This should give pause to those who have suspected the authenticity of the inscription on the Guido Polyptych. It is possible a tradition existed for inscriptions on these long, low panels; certainly the ample space along the bottom invited such treatment. By contrast, not one of the Madonnas Enthroned by Guido and his shop can reliably be said to have been inscribed from the time of execution. This lends credence to the suggestion that the inscription of the Palazzo Pubblico *Madonna* was taken from this Polyptych. It is not at all credible that the borrowing could have been the reverse, as is supposed by Weigelt, van Marle, and Brandi.

This panel is entirely by Guido himself, one of the few panels about which there can be no question. It is of the highest quality and despite the damages it has suffered, offers an excellent view of Guido working on a large scale. Since so much of the Palazzo Pubblico *Madonna* has been lost, the No. 7 Polyptych is an invaluable help in studying the style of Guido. All the more wonder, then, that the criticism of this painting has been so harsh. The inability to distinguish qualitatively between this and the other Guidesque Polyptych, No. 6 in the Siena Pinacoteca (Fig. 33), is a reminder of the poor stylistic analysis to which Guido's art has, by and large, been subjected. A sampling of these views is in order. Brandi, Venturi, Sandberg-Vavalà, Weigelt, and Longhi express the belief that the No. 7 is inferior to the No. 6. Brandi uses the No. 7 to demonstrate how the style of Guido's remote followers had fallen "nel più basso grado di barbarismo." Offner, on the other hand, has made a perceptive analysis of the place of this masterpiece in Guido's oeuvre.

Even a cursory examination should erase the notion that this is an inferior work of the shop of Guido. We may begin by noticing how well-placed the figures are in their compartments; it should not be difficult to see that the arrangement is subtler than in the No. 6 Polyptych where the Madonna is too large in proportion to the surrounding figures. The silhouettes in the No. 7 Polyptych, so nicely adjusted to one another, establish the quality and sensitivity of this painting. But the differences can only be appreciated when the nature of Guido's style becomes clear. His is an incisively linear style with crisp overlappings of forms and tonalities and an awareness of the juxtaposition of dark solids against the shimmering gold ground. We cannot appreciate the rhythm of this painting at its fullest inasmuch as the two lateral compartments have been sawn off, but we can glimpse it partially. The slightly inclined heads and the movement generated by the various gestures act to unify the composition and draw the clearly isolated figures together.

A study of the rich variety of designs on the tunic, the mantle, and the headcloth of the Madonna (Fig. 8), and the carefully wrought patterns etched onto them reveals the craftsmanship of Guido at its best. This sort of craftsmanship was to become an important feature in all later Sienese painting.

All the faces of this Polyptych have personality. This is especially true of the Madonna (Fig. 9) and the Mary Magdalen who begin to suggest something of that charm for which Sienese painting was to be famous. By contrast, the Madonna of the No. 6 Polyptych (Fig. 41) is round-faced and mechanical, and the attendant saints are country cousins of those in the Polyptych by Guido. By some alchemy of the painter the figures in the No. 7 panel, which have none of the advantages of the naturalism of a later age, manage to communicate a lively sentiment to the spectator.

The face of St. Francis (Fig. 69) reminds us that this is still an age in which an idea can be conveyed in a quasi-abstract manner: his face is a mask of the ascetic. The gaunt physical quality of the face is produced by symmetrical swinging arcs on the cheeks, while his otherworldly nature is conveyed by the embroidery of lines around the eyes and on the forehead.

The attribution of the Polyptych No. 7 to Guido, based to a large extent on the general aesthetic of the composition, the shapes and relationships of the figures, and the concepts of linear rhythms, is also and ultimately premised on an identity of forms between these figures and the indisputably original parts of the Palazzo Pubblico *Madonna*. The similarities abound, as, for instance, in the Christ Child (Fig. 66) of the Polyptych and the spandrel angels (Fig. 65) of the Palazzo Pubblico panel where we find the same full, fleshy head and face, thick, woolly strands of hair, full lips, and flicker of animation around the eyes. The similarities between the Magdalen and the Evangelist of the Polyptych (Fig. 7) and the right-hand angel (Fig. 15) of the Palazzo Pubblico gable are striking. The Christ (Fig. 68) of the gable is a modification of the St. Francis (Fig. 69) of the Polyptych; the treatment of the beards, for example, is identical.

A number of things indicate the earliness of this Polyptych in relation to the Palazzo Pubblico *Madonna*. The frame is not so fully developed in its system of moldings, and the figure of the Christ Child expresses little of that mobility so impressive in the later work. It seems reasonable to imagine that the missing part of the inscription on the right concluded with a date in the early 1270's; an interval of eight to ten years between this panel and the Palazzo Pubblico *Madonna* may properly be supposed.

BIBLIOGRAPHY

1859 Biadi, Bib. 18, p. 303.
1865 Brogi, Bib. 24 (pub. 1897), p. 159.
1895 Lisini, Bib. 96, p. 10.
1895 Siena, Bib. 160, p. 6.

1897 Brogi, Bib. 24, p. 159.
1903 Douglas, Bib. 60, p. 164 n. 3.
1903 Siena, Bib. 161, p. 5.
1907 Venturi, Bib. 188, pp. 47, 49-50.
1907 Jacobsen, Bib. 85, p. 11.
1911 Weigelt, Bib. 191, pp. 219, 222, 227
1920 Marle, Bib. 110, p. 269.
1920 Berenson, Bib. 16, pp. 260-61.
1922 Weigelt, Bib. 192, p. 281.
1923 Marle, Bib. 107, I, pp. 372, 377.
1928 Weigelt, Bib. 195, pp. 203-8.
1931 Brandi, Bib. 22, pp. 77-78.
1932 Berenson, Bib. 15, p. 269.
1932 Edgell, Bib. 61, pp. 28, 31, 34.
1933 Siena, Bib. 164, pp. 118-19.

1933 Brandi, Bib. 21, p. 3.
1934 Sandberg-Vavalà, Bib. 151, pp. 259-62, 267, 268.
1943 *Giottesca*, Bib. 167, pp. 90-91.
1947 Garrison, Bib. 74, p. 303.
1948 Longhi, Bib. 100, p. 36.
1949 Garrison, Bib. 73, p. 165 and No. 430.
1950 Offner, Bib. 133, pp. 62, 63, 65, 67, 68, 78.
1953 Sandberg-Vavalà, Bib. 153, pp. 23, 34-36.
1955 Carli, Bib. 28, pp. 20, 24.
1958 Siena, Bib. 165, p. 15.
1959 Stubblebine, Bib. 175, p. 267.

III. *Lenten Hanging: Transfiguration, Entry into Jerusalem, Raising of Lazarus*

FIGURES 10-13   Siena Pinacoteca No. 8   H 90 x W 186 cm.

The painting is on linen and has a very thin coat of gesso priming. There is no indication that the linen was ever backed by a panel (see below). There are scattered damages, the worst being in the robes of Christ in each scene. There are faint horizontal fracture lines, especially at the level of Christ's waist in the *Entry into Jerusalem* and the *Raising of Lazarus*. The decorative scroll between the scenes probably also went around the edges originally.

There are two inscriptions: at the top of the *Transfiguration*: ELIAS MOYSES; at the top of the *Entry into Jerusalem*: ENTRATA IN GERUSALEMME (possibly a later addition).

The painting came to the Siena Pinacoteca from the Pieve di Santa Cecilia, Crevole, in 1894. Its earlier history is unknown.

This painting is from the hand of Guido.

A number of problems are posed when one considers what function the painting could have served. To begin with, the thirteenth century is so much the age of panel painting that any exception is remarkable. It has usually been assumed that this work must at one time have been painted on a wooden panel and subsequently transferred to canvas. However, if this was originally a linen painting, we should expect to find some evidence of the fact in what we see before us and this should help determine the purpose for which the painting was executed. Such evidence is visible in the fracture lines which do not seem to have been caused by breaks in an underlying wood panel but by the rolling up of the fabric. This would have been the case if the painting were used only occasionally and stored between times.

The explanation for such a usage can be found in an examination of the scenes themselves. To begin with, the three scenes do not follow one another in chronological order; reading them historically one would proceed from the Transfiguration to the Raising of Lazarus to the Entry into Jerusalem. In no other representation is the order transposed as in this painting.

It is also to be noted that the scenes are unusually isolated from one another, having little narrative flow or continuity; neither rocks, architecture nor figures carry the action from one episode to another. Furthermore, the *Entry* is wider than the other scenes and this, taken with the fact that it is shifted out of chronological order, suggests to us that the *Entry* is intended to be the focal point of the painting. This is also confirmed by the strong central axis in the *Entry*; the figure of Christ on the ass is foiled by the pyramidal hill, by the two flanking hills, and by the cross-shaped palm.

It may be said that this painting consists of three hieratic and iconic pictures, rather than a sequence of three events related in time and place. It may be significant that the city in the *Entry* is perched far away on a hill in the upper right whereas we usually find it close at hand with an emphasis on the gate through which Christ is to proceed, as in Duccio's *Maestà*. The important element is the figure of Christ on the ass; important too are the welcoming crowds and the palms. The reference to Palm Sunday processions is inescapable. Now we know that in Germany of the late Middle Ages wood sculptures of Christ on the ass were pulled along on wheels in Palm Sunday processions. There is also a record of a stuffed donkey in Verona which probably served a similar purpose (Bib. 136). Such an emphasis on Christ on the ass as a part of Palm Sunday celebration makes us wonder whether our painting may have been intended for display on Palm Sunday, or during Holy Week, or, even, throughout Lent. Although very little is known of Lenten practices in Italy, we have more information from the north of Europe. Certain hangings of the late Middle Ages, such as the *Paremont de Narbonne*, were designed specifically for a Lenten use; the latter's subdued, gray color and the representations of Passion scenes are appropriate to the season of penitence (Bib. 172).

While Brandi (Bib. 164) and Weigelt (Bib. 194) think of the Guidesque painting as an antependium, or hanging for the front of an altar, and Venturi (Bib. 188) thinks it may have adorned a tomb monument, it seems more plausible that it was brought out during Lent to cover a regular altarpiece. With the Entry into Jerusalem, the events of Passion Week are inaugurated. The flanking scenes of this work represent two very different kinds of miracles and these contain intimations of immortality appropriate to the Easter period. The color certainly corroborates such an idea; the preponderance of cool greens and the absence of any brilliant hues give the work a hushed and subdued quality not found in any other Guidesque work. This too suggests the suitability of the painting for Lenten use.

The landscape mood of the *Entry into Jerusalem* is due in large part to the delicate patterns of greenery with which the scene is festooned. The abundance of trees and branches and the wide, handsome bands of vine scrolls which separate the scenes, and probably served as a border around the edge, give a tapestry-like effect. And in fact, the aesthetic of this painting is not very different from that of tapestries. This is due also to the unusually even distribution of forms over the entire surface. Thus, such a painting on linen, flexible and easily moved about, would have served admirably as a seasonal hanging.

A stylistic analysis relates these festival scenes to the Badia Ardenga narratives and to the spandrel angels of the Palazzo Pubblico *Madonna*, making an attribution to Guido demonstrable. The *Entry into Jerusalem* (Fig. 12) is painted with an unabashed pictorialism. Each section of the rock formations is carefully articulated with thin, white lines which model them and define their round or sharp edges. In the Badia Ardenga scenes, especially the *Adoration* (Fig. 21), the *Flight into Egypt* (Fig. 22) and the *Entombment* (Fig. 30), the rocks become mountains; they are placed well behind the figures and assume more rugged, monumental proportions. This is a matter of Guido's development; by the time he paints the Badia Ardenga narratives, he will have moved away from the miniaturistic concepts of the Lenten Hanging. The difference, in fact, helps us to date the Lenten Hanging in a period some years before the Badia Ardenga scenes. Despite the limitations of his earlier manner, Guido is remarkably successful in the lyrical landscape of the *Entry into Jerusalem* and the visionary mood of the *Transfiguration*.

The architecture of the three scenes is also analogous to that in the Badia Ardenga scenes. The Lazarus scene (Fig. 13) is the closest; it may be compared to the *Adoration* (Fig. 21) where there is a similar combination of a boxlike building placed behind a low, sloping building. The color and texture of the surfaces, the type and combination of the fenestrations, the cornices, and the thin, black and white lines between stories are identical. There are differences, to be sure, as can be seen in the more realistic sense of forms in space in the Badia Ardenga scenes, but this is the result of the time interval and the development of the artist. One important factor in this development is the influence of Cimabue with his remarkable interest in three-dimensional objects and definition of spaces; this influence was evidently not available to Guido when he painted the Reliquary Shutters.

The correspondence of the Lenten Hanging to the later works of Guido extends to the figure style. The type of the youthful, male head seen in the Evangelist on the left of the *Transfiguration* (Fig. 11) and in a number of faces in the *Entry into Jerusalem* (Fig. 67) has both the physiognomy and the personality, robust and intense, of the spandrel angels (Fig. 65) in the Palazzo Pubblico panel. The type is present in the *Raising of Lazarus* in Lazarus and the youth standing next to him. Such analogies are also found in the representations of Christ. The soft, luminous effects around the chin and that expression which is at once austere and benign are the same as we find in the Christ in the *Crucifixion* (Fig. 28) from the Badia Ardenga group and, on a vastly larger scale, the Redeemer (Fig. 68) of the pediment in the Palazzo Pubblico.

As for other types, there is a correspondence between the bearded St. James in the lower right of the *Transfiguration* and the king on the left of the *Adoration* (Fig. 21). Again, it is Cimabue who must have provided the example of this figural style or, to put it more precisely, made a new influx of Byzantinism available to other Tuscan artists. The tall, graceful figures and the more painterly modeling of the features distinguish the figures of the Lenten Hanging from those of the Reliquary Shutters, just as Cimabue's figures may be distinguished from those of Coppo di Marcovaldo.

Perhaps the drapery provides the clearest demonstration of the same authorship of the Lenten Hanging and the Badia Ardenga scenes. That line and pattern which dynamize the draperies of the Annunciate Angel (Fig. 18), the figures of the *Nativity* (Fig. 20), and the angels of the spandrels (Fig. 17), are discovered throughout this work too: most particularly in the St. John and St. Peter of the *Transfiguration*. The drapery, like the details of the figures and the landscape, is more detailed and tighter in execution than those in the other, later work. By the time of the Badia Ardenga scenes Guido had learned a great deal about simplifying and monumentalizing both figures and compositions. From the foregoing, it appears that the Lenten Hanging is a work executed in the decade before the San Domenico Altarpiece of the 1280's. It is far more mature than the Reliquary Shutters No. 4 which we believe he painted around 1260. The Lenten Hanging, therefore, must be dated at some time in the early 1270's.

BIBLIOGRAPHY

1895 Siena, Bib. 160, p. 6.	1927 Toesca, Bib. 182, 1, p. 1038 n. 44.
1903 Siena, Bib. 161, p. 6.	1930 Weigelt, Bib. 194, pp. 2, 12, 103.
1907 Venturi, Bib. 188, v, p. 110.	1932 Berenson, Bib. 15, p. 269.
1907 Jacobsen, Bib. 85, pp. 11, 14.	1933 Siena, Bib. 164, p. 112.
1911 Weigelt, Bib. 191, pp. 25, 225-26.	1939 Bacci, Bib. 7, p. 29.
1916 Millet, Bib. 121, p. xlvii.	1949 Garrison, Bib. 73, No. 414.
1920 Marle, Bib. 110, p. 269.	1953 Sandberg-Vavalà, Bib. 153, p. 49.
1924 Siena, Bib. 163, p. 10.	1956 Fisher, Bib. 65, p. 51.
1927 Offner, Bib. 134, p. 37.	1958 Siena, Bib. 165, p. 11.

IV. *San Domenico Altarpiece*
a) *Palazzo Pubblico Madonna*
b) *Palazzo Pubblico Gable: Redeemer and Two Angels*
c) *Badia Ardenga Narratives: The Infancy and Passion of Christ*

IVa. *Palazzo Pubblico Madonna*

FIGURES 14, 17, 19, 70, 71, 73   Siena, Palazzo Pubblico   H 283 x W 194 cm.

The panel was almost entirely repainted at the time of a refurbishing in the shop of Duccio in the early fourteenth century. The angels in the spandrels are more or less intact except for superficial damages. X rays at the time of the cleaning in 1949 revealed that the face of the Madonna and Child had been scraped away before the repainting; this also proved true of the left side of the throne and its lower part. From beneath the Cosmatesque style of throne added by Duccio's shop there have appeared on the right side parts of a throne in the Dugento style, composed of large, cup-shaped leaves and protruding horizontal bands. Removal of the repaint has revealed the original headcloth of the Madonna with its system of delicate gold striations. It was not possible, of course, to take away the repainting of the two principal faces or the veil which falls around the Madonna's throat, or the left side of the throne, since nothing of the original remains beneath these parts. Removal of the Ducciesque right hand of the Madonna has brought to light the familiar Guidesque hand with its long fingers tapering almost to points. In restoring the right hand of the Madonna a vestige of the Ducciesque index finger was left outlined against the dark mantle, a memento, both amusing and disturbing, of the fourteenth century refurbishing and the twentieth century restoration.

Along the bottom of the panel, partly on the edge of the footstool, and then turning up along the diagonal side of the footstool at the right, the following inscription can be read:

✠ ME GUIDO DE SENIS DIEBUS DEPINXIT AMENIS: QUEM X̄R̄S LENIS NULLIS

VELIT AGERE PENIS AÑO · D · M̊ · CCXXI

The question of the authenticity of this inscription and, therefore, of the 1221 date, long a subject of debate, will be discussed below. Here, it need only be mentioned that following the recent restoration Brandi (Bib. 23) concluded that the inscription is contemporary with the rest of the painting. His evidence is the discovery that the pink of the undergarment laps over the blue ground of the inscription at one point and that one of the gold striations of that garment runs down over a part of the lettering. Certain as we are that the inscription has nothing to do with the original painting and that, in any case, 1221 is an inacceptable date on stylistic grounds, we must assume that the garment was at least touched up during the fourteenth century overhauling.

The *Madonna* and its pediment have been in the Sala del Mappamondo of the Palazzo Pubblico since 1888. In 1864 Crowe and Cavalcaselle (Bib. 46) saw the painting in San Domenico but they noted that the gable had been placed in the Convent Church of San Domenico. In 1859 Milanesi (Bib. 120) saw the *Madonna* in San Domenico; his silence in regard to the gable indicates it had already been separated from the *Madonna*. However, in 1827 Rumohr (Bib. 146) saw the *Madonna* together with its gable in the Venturini Chapel of San Domenico. It was there that the painting was seen by Padre Della Valle (Bib. 56) in 1782 and by Gigli (Bib. 80) in 1723. We know from the *Chronotaxis* of Carapelli (see Bib. 120) that the painting was placed in the Venturini Chapel in 1705. Before that time it had been hung above the principal door of San Domenico, on the interior. In that high place it was seen by Montfaucon (Bib. 123) in 1702, by Ugurgieri (Bib. 185) in 1649, and by Fabio Chigi (see Bib. 9) in 1625. In the 1520's Sigismondo Tizio (see Bib 20) describes the *Madonna* as being in the Capacci Chapel of the same church. It was probably removed from that chapel to the position above the main door in 1600, the date of the Francesco Vanni Altarpiece that seems to have replaced it.

The passage in Tizio mentioned above, which is from volume ten of his manuscript *History of Siena,* is of considerable importance for the early history of the *Madonna,* and has been quoted frequently in the Guido literature. To begin with, Tizio declares that the painting had been made for the nearby, older church of San Gregorio, a church which was demolished later in the thirteenth century (for discussions of this see Bib. 75, Bib. 20). Tizio must have observed the discrepancy between the 1221 date and the erection of San Domenico during the later course of the thirteenth century. As a matter of fact, old documents, still known in the eighteenth century, indicated that San Gregorio was turned over to the Dominicans sometime around 1240 so that they might carry out their functions while awaiting the completion of their own new church (Bib. 20, p. 105). Tizio must have assumed that the painting was afterwards transferred to San Domenico.

Tizio also locates the painting as being in a chapel just to the left as you enter San Domenico, identifying it as the Capacci Chapel. He then tells us that the painting is of an ancient style, and he quotes the inscription with its date. Finally, he relates that this *Madonna* is only part of a larger work: the two wings that once closed over the *Madonna* were in his time hung high up on the wall as you proceed on into the church. The passage reads as follows:

> Fuerat olim in Senensi urbe divi Gregorii parrochialis ecclesia in Campo Regio, cuius sane structura muris vetustis adhuc cernitur secus turrim sonantem (campanile quidem vocant) apud divi Dominici fratres. Ea enim, ut in nostris historiis tradidimus, cura et populo ad Sanctum Antonium et Egidium translatis, Predicatoribus religiosis fratribus concessa fuit. In eiusdem ecclesie maioris ara tabula cum Virginis imagine priscorum more depicta fuerat, dicata anno salutis ducentesimo vigesimo primo supra millesimum, cum huiusmodi verbibus in inferiori parte tabulae descriptis: Me Guido de Senis diebus depinxit amoenis,
>
> Quem Christus lenis nullis velit agere poenis.
>
> Ea enim tabula ad laevam mox cum ingrederis Sancti Dominici aedem in Capacciorum cappella conspicitur: aliae vero duae quae Virginem utroque latere olim claudebant, cum in ecclesiam sursum progrederis ad parietes tibi sese offerunt.

The curious form of the word *aliae*, wings, is a Tuscan fifteenth century combination of the Italian *ali* and the Latin *alae*; this was brought to my attention by Miss Giulia Brunetti.

Tizio talks about the *Madonna* in another part of the *History*, volume one, but what he says there is curiously different and it leads, very probably, to what may be the earliest mention of the Guido *Madonna*. In contrast to the description of the painting in volume ten, which bespeaks his familiarity with the work *in situ*, the reference in volume one in an offhand manner makes an association between the *Madonna* and the date of December 17, 1221. "1221. die insuper decembris anni huius decima septima. . . ." It sounds, indeed, as though he had just taken this information from some written source. The specific date of December 17 recalls the passage in the so-called Agnolo di Tura Chronicle, a manuscript of the fifteenth century which speaks of an altarpiece made in Siena and finished on December 17, 1221, for the church of San Domenico and which was to the left just inside the door (a location which Tizio later identified as the Capacci Chapel). The passage further relates that the work was a venerated and beautiful image and that there was a connection with the Malavolti family. (For a discussion of the passage see Bib. 75.) The sentence runs as follows:

> 1221. Una tavola d'altare fu fatta in Siena la quale fu finita e messa adi 17 di dicembre 1221. ne chiesa di sandomenico in canpo regi acanto ala porta dentro a mano mancha ede molto devota e bella . . . de malavolti.

Unfortunately, the part of the Tura manuscript in which the Guido *Madonna* is mentioned is known only in two eighteenth century copies. We have no certain evidence that the passage was in the original, fifteenth century manuscript and is not an interpolation of the eighteenth century. The very fact, though, that Tizio mentions a specific day, December 17, suggests he knew an earlier written record of the *Madonna*, and this very well may have been the Tura manuscript. If so, we can trace the Guido *Madonna* back to the fifteenth century.

There is no way of proving that such a fifteenth century passage was based on earlier documents, but the strong likelihood exists there was fact become legend before that time. The sentiment of the Tura passage suggests that the venerability and fame of the *Madonna* were not new.

The Palazzo Pubblico *Madonna* is important as the central and principal part of Guido's most ambitious undertaking, the Altarpiece for the high altar of the great, new church of San Domenico in Siena. It also inaugurates a wholly new Guidesque formula for the representation of the Madonna Enthroned, and serves as the prototype for a number of shop variants made in the next several decades. Many things have changed from his earlier formula of the 1270's, a formula exemplified by the San Bernardino and Arezzo *Madonnas* (Figs. 31, 32).

Guido introduces into the panel, apparently for the first time in Italian painting, the graceful device of the cusped arch above an enthroned Madonna (Fig. 14). In the Palazzo Pubblico *Madonna* the cusped arch governs the composition; its cadence is picked up in the head and halo of the Madonna, in the halo of the Child, and in the rhythmic curve of the white maphorium under the Child. The Madonna accommodates herself to the curve of the arch with the bend of her head. The single arc of the throneback becomes a counterpoint to it. As an important element of the new formula for the Madonna Enthroned, the cusped arch is used in all examples that follow, with the exception of the late *Madonna* in the Kraków Tabernacle. Duccio was surely sensitive to this new compositional device even though he never uses the Guidesque scheme; still the arcs of the throneback in his Rucellai *Madonna* (Fig. 125) establish a similar cadence across that panel. Popular again with Simone Martini (Fig. 78), the cusped arch is ubiquitous in the fourteenth century.

Guido also introduces angels above the cusped arch, three in each spandrel. This was not a new motif; in the Polyptych No. 6 (Fig. 33) angels were placed over the arches between each figure, but they established no communication with the figures in the compartments below. In the Palazzo Pubblico *Madonna* the lively angels, perched in their own celestial sphere, gaze down rapturously at the Madonna and Child, abolishing as they do so the barrier of the arch. It is an invention which is taken up many times in later Sienese painting.

A new type of chair-throne appears in the Palazzo Pubblico *Madonna*, probably adapted from the chair-throne which Cimabue introduced into the stream of Dugento Tuscan painting in the 1270's in his fresco of the Madonna with St. Francis (Fig. 72) in the lower church at Assisi or in another lost prototype. The throne of the Palazzo Pubblico *Madonna* can be reconstructed (Fig. 73), partly as a result of the removal of repaint from the right side (Fig. 71), and partly from the reflections of it in the Florence and Galli-Dunn *Madonnas* (Figs. 39, 43). Whereas the throne in earlier panels had consisted of an impenetrable block of decorative motifs, such as the un-broken bands of leaf patterns in the Arezzo panel (Fig. 32), the new style has perforations of small arcades and some suggestions of wood-lathed parts. The seat of the throne now recedes more horizontally than before and there are finials at the front corners of the seat which establish a forward plane behind which the forms take on a new three-dimensional reality.

Just as important are the innovations in the figures of the Madonna and Child. The Child leans back and gazes up at his mother so that the rigidity and formality which had previously emphasized his role as Redeemer is largely abandoned. The blessing gesture, so pronounced in the earlier formula, is almost lost sight of as he bends his arm in towards his chest. In the earlier Madonna panels the Madonna had grasped the maphorium spread beneath the Child; now she grasps the Child under his arm, producing a novel sense of his physical presence. This more human rela-tionship between the Madonna and Child exceeds by far the tentative efforts in this direction taken by Coppo di Marcovaldo in his Siena *Madonna* (Fig. 80) of 1261; at the same time it is only a step to the development in Duccio's Rucellai *Madonna* (Fig. 125).

The Palazzo Pubblico *Madonna* is filled with a wealth of sumptuous detail: the angular, zigzagging gold hems which counterpoint the curvilinear movements of the haloes and the cusped arch, the rich patterns of the cushion and drapery behind the throne, and above all, the decorations of the haloes. The halo of the Madonna (Fig. 17) is the most elaborate and imaginative in all Guidesque painting and foreshadows closely the effects achieved by Duccio in his Rucellai *Madonna*. Filled with flowers, leaves, stalks and geometric shapes of the subtlest and most delicate workmanship, it contrasts vividly with the brusquer incisions of his Florentine contemporary, Cimabue. (The decorative system is discussed in Offner, Bib. 133, pp. 77-80; see also Weigelt, Bib. 194, p. 2.)

The Palazzo Pubblico *Madonna* marks a milestone in Sienese painting. It surpasses the earlier style of the Enthroned Madonna developed by Guido himself and, while dependent on certain innovations of Cimabue, exudes a wholly Sienese flavor. It is interesting that in 1702 the French traveler, Padre Bernard de Montfaucon, writing in his *Diarium italicum*, is impressed with such graceful delineation in a work done in that time of primitive picture-making. When he uses the word *elegantia*, the painting and the painter are for the first time characterized as intrinsically Sienese.

Finally, the very scale of the Palazzo Pubblico *Madonna* is impressive, even without the parts which must have flanked it on the sides and above in its altarpiece form. As Offner (Bib. 133) has pointed out, the statistics emphasize rather precisely the place of Guido in the development of Tuscan painting in the second half of the thirteenth century. The Palazzo Pubblico *Madonna* with its gable has a height of 362 cm. by a width of 194 cm. and far surpasses Coppo's 1261 *Madonna*, H 220 x W 125, which in Guido's earlier period must have seemed so grand. Guido is closer to Cimabue's Trinita *Madonna* of the 1290's, H 385 x W 223, but he has not reached the dizzying heights of Duccio's Rucellai *Madonna*, H 450 x W 290 cm.

Our stylistic analysis of the Palazzo Pubblico *Madonna* demonstrates very clearly that it cannot be a work of the early part of the thirteenth century. The size alone prohibits such an idea. But more specifically, the relationship to Cimabue and the borrowing of such Cimabuesque compositional devices as the view of the diagonal side of the chair-throne, tell us within rather narrow time limits when Guido was working. The human relationship Guido sets up between the figures has no counterpart in the early Dugento or, for that matter, in Coppo di Marcovaldo. The sophistication of such elements as the cusped arch, the moldings of the frame, and the design of the haloes, all belong to a late part of the century and, indeed, have no relevance to early thirteenth century style. In all this analysis the 1221 date has no significance whatever.

Nonetheless, nothing in the entire literature on Guido has elicited so much debate as the question of the authenticity of the inscription and the early date of 1221 contained therein. The early opinions both pro and con are a matter of purely historical interest inasmuch as both sides were quite blind to the nature of thirteenth century painting. As we now know, the face of the Madonna was masked by a more modern one a number of years later in the shop of Duccio. Of such obstacles our early writers were blissfully unaware so that the face was taken as evidence of Guido's precociousness. The Florentines were talking in the dark insofar as they cited the Rucellai *Madonna*, then in Santa Maria Novella, as a principal work by Cimabue, whereas we now know that it is a work of the Sienese artist, Duccio. If our early writers seem parlous, they should perhaps be forgiven; the situation was full of anomalies which civic pride would never allow them to explore.

Certainly it was patriotic considerations that led to the famous feud between the Florentines and the Sienese over the locus of the revival of painting in the thirteenth century; standards were taken up either for Cimabue of Florence or Guido of Siena. If, for instance, Vasari had mentioned the Palazzo Pubblico *Madonna* with its strikingly early date, he would have been hard put to justify his claims about the priority of Cimabue and the city of Florence in the resurgence of the arts. Giulio Mancini (Bib. 105), native of Siena, physician to Pope Urban VIII, and celebrated writer on the arts, gives the inscription without, however, setting down the 1221 date and, curiously, mentioning the date of 1240 whenever he speaks of Guido and the *Madonna*. Mancini marvels over the fact that Vasari says nothing about Guido when, clearly, the revival of the art of painting had taken place before Cimabue was born. And then Baldinucci (Bib. 12), writing on the subject of the revival of painting without so much as mentioning the name of Guido, accuses Mancini of "una gran passione contro il Vasari."

Although the 1221 date was considered prima-facie evidence by most Sienese writers, some sought to establish the priority of Siena without leaning too heavily on that single dated work, the San Domenico *Madonna*. Thus Isidoro Ugurgieri in his *Pompe Sanesi* (Bib. 185) of 1649 turns up the information that a Sienese painter, "Diotisalvi Pittore," was an important personage already in 1256, so that quite evidently painting was important in Siena before Cimabue was born. Ugurgieri accuses Vasari of partiality towards the Florentines and in this he is far more prideful and militant than Mancini. And unlike Mancini he actually says something about the painting itself when he calls it "molto maestosa."

The Florentines met the Sienese arguments with a curious rationalization, the substance of which is reported to us by the Padre Bernard de Montfaucon in his *Diarium italicum* (Bib. 123) of 1702. The 1221 *Madonna*, so the Florentines argue, is the only work which Guido has left and it has no great merit. Furthermore, Guido did not train any followers whereas Cimabue, who has left many pictures, had a number of disciples who gradually brought art to perfection. Guido's *Madonna*, then, is conceived of as a chance occurrence and its author hardly deserves credit for the revivification of the arts. Perhaps as a result of the great debate Girolamo Gigli in his *Diario Sanese* of 1723 describes the San Domenico *Madonna* as one of the most famous pictures in all Italy. His stock phrase is "prima che fiorisse Cimabue," that is, before Cimabue flourished.

From the writings of the Sienese historian, Uberto Benvoglienti (1668-1733), mostly in manuscript form (see Bib. 56), we have a novel appraisal of Guido and his famous work. The question of a possible repainting of the *Madonna* having arisen, the painter Giuseppe Nasini quickly assured Benvoglienti that this was not the case. It is the first time this factor entered the discussion. Nasini also told Benvoglienti that Guido worked "outside of the old Greek style." Elsewhere one wonders about the reliability of Benvoglienti. He quotes Mancini as referring to a Guido Fiori who lived before Giotto and who painted ca. 1221 in a "maniera non greca." None of these assertions are to be found in Mancini; rather, it all sounds suspiciously like the advice of Benvoglienti's painter friend, Nasini.

The early phase of Guido criticism culminates with Padre Della Valle's *Lettere senesi* (Bib. 56) of 1782. Evidently Della Valle had done considerable research on the matter of Guido and the San Domenico *Madonna* to judge by the many quotations from Tizio, Mancini, Benvoglienti, and Montfaucon, besides all of his own observations. While he follows the old battle lines on some points, praising Guido at the expense of Cimabue and believing in the authenticity of the 1221 date, he also searched the archives for references to painters named Guido, attempting to associate the painter of the *Madonna* with one or another painter of that name mentioned in old documents.

In Sienese writings of the seventeenth and eighteenth centuries Guido gradually emerged as a semi-legendary hero, founder not only of Sienese painting but the one who revived the arts in Italy. The proud Florentines were never very happy about the situation. Yet it was not so important an issue to them as it was to the Sienese who, ever more provincial, relied ever more on the old myth.

With the nineteenth century the body of literature on Guido becomes so voluminous that only major viewpoints can be mentioned. A number of critics followed Milanesi's opinion of 1859 (Bib. 120) that the inscription must originally have read 1281. Many others continued, however, to believe in the authenticity of the inscription and the 1221 date. In the twentieth century the growing awareness of the disparity between the date of 1221 and the period in which Guido must have worked has resulted from a more scientific approach to the problem.

A brief review of the opinions of the last few decades is in order. Sandberg-Vavalà in 1934 (Bib. 151) had said that we are "bound to face the remote date of 1221 and adjust our theorizing, as best we can, to this difficult fact." By 1953 (Bib. 153) the same critic could urge that "the 1221 date is to be laid aside as a deliberate error of the Ducciesque restorer made with intent to augment the antiquity of the already venerable and venerated picture." In 1955 Carli (Bib. 28) found it difficult to sustain the 1221 date because of the many correspondences to dated or datable works in the second half of the century. Oertel (Bib. 128) speaks of Guido as working between 1260-80 and as influenced by Coppo di Marcovaldo and concurs with Carli that the 1221 date must have been taken by Guido from an earlier Madonna. In 1957 Coor (Bib. 40) referred to Guido as "the leading Sienese painter in the seventh and eighth decades of the thirteenth century," basing her argument on a complex of influences from other artists of that time. Meiss (Bib. 115) indicates an activity of the shop in the 1270's. Garrison in 1949 (Bib. 73) gave a date of ca. 1270 for the Palazzo Pubblico *Madonna,* saying that all the evidence "compels a dating in the third quarter of the century." In 1950 Offner (Bib. 133) indicated a date of about 1281 for the *Madonna,* arriving by a methodical study of stylistic factors at the same date Milanesi had proposed. On the other hand, Brandi (Bib. 20 and Bib. 23) still finds Guido an artist of rustic simplicity from the early thirteenth century, believing the 1221 date original and suited to the painting style of the Palazzo Pubblico *Madonna.* Thus, in the last dozen years a preponderance of critics have tended to favor the period 1270-90 for the work of Guido.

The growing tendency toward a later dating of the Palazzo Pubblico *Madonna* has been paralleled by an increasing number of hypotheses that have been proposed to explain the presence of the inscription with its 1221 date. One major trend has its ancestry in Milanesi who suggested that an L was lost after the MCC, and that an x was lost after the xx, thus giving an original reading of MCCLXXXI (1281). As an alternate suggestion, Milanesi suggested a c was dropped after the xx, thus giving an original reading of MCCXXCI (1281). Lusini (Bib. 101), by a similar restoration of lost numerals, arrived at an original date of MCCXXXXI (1241). Van Marle (Bib. 107), misquoting Milanesi's proposal, says an L is missing and thereby arrives at the date MCCLXXI (1271). Edgell, quoting Milanesi, makes the same mistake van Marle had, arriving at the incorrect date of 1271. Coletti (Bib. 35) suggests a reading of MCCLXI (1261). Garrison (Bib. 73) proposes that the date should read MCCCXXI (1321) and that the inscription commemorates not the creation of the painting but rather its Duccieque restoration. Carli (Bib. 26) has suggested that the inscription is copied from an older image which Guido's *Madonna* replaced, and in this suggestion he has been seconded by Oertel (Bib. 128).

The inscription no longer seems so enigmatic. The remarkable similarity between the wording on the Polyptych No. 7 and that on the Palazzo Pubblico *Madonna* leads one to believe that the fourteenth century restorer of the *Madonna* took the inscription quite literally from the Polyptych, only changing the date. This would account for the way, strange already in 1864 to Crowe and Cavalcaselle (Bib. 46), the close of the inscription runs up along the diagonal right side of the footstool (Fig. 71). Offner (Bib. 133) has pointed out the unorthodox manner in which the inscription begins against the void to the left (Fig. 70). Apparently the restorer was attempting to fit all the words into a space for which they were never designed. Offner has also noted such curiosities as the unusual contraction of the "anno domini" and the awkward placing of the "M" of the date. After these precautions, designed to save space, the restorer then found an empty area at the very end which he filled with a rather irrelevant leaf-flourish. The anomalous placing of the footstool in a perspective just the reverse of that of the throne above it contradicts the system followed in all other Dugento representations. The conclusion is inescapable that the restorer, faced with adapting a borrowed verse from a horizontal panel to the relatively narrow limits of the Palazzo Pubblico *Madonna,* painted a new footstool and even then had to write part of the wording on empty space and along two sides of the footstool without giving any thought to the proprieties in such matters.

Everything militates against Tizio's notion, defended by some, that the painting could have been intended for the old parish church of San Gregorio. The idea must have suggested itself because of the discrepancy between the date of San Domenico and that on the painting; it was only in 1225 that steps were taken toward a church building for the Dominicans. At that time Fortebraccio Malavolta gave land for the project at the spot known as the Campo Reggio. The building history of San Domenico is given in Lusini (Bib. 103). We gather from the records that the building was far from finished in 1244 and as late as 1262 an allocation of funds had to be made for this purpose. When what appears to have been a catafalque for the recently deceased Beato Ambrogio Sansedoni was set up "nel bel mezzo" of San Domenico in 1286, we may assume the interior was already sufficiently complete to house a sizable altarpiece.

In any case, only by that time in the century would such an altarpiece have been possible. As P. Mandonnet (Bib. 106) points out: "During a great part of the thirteenth century the [Dominican] Order prohibited all decoration or interior ornamentation of churches." Only as the century wore on did the Order give in to the inevitable. Thus, both the building history of the Dominican church in Siena and the earlier, austere tastes of that Order combine to preclude the possibility that an altarpiece would have been ordered earlier than 1280. Everything else indicates that this is just about when the Palazzo Pubblico *Madonna* was painted.

It has been suggested above that the 1221 date inscribed on the Palazzo Pubblico *Madonna,* far from being an inadvertence or mistake, very probably had a specific import. In 1705 Giuseppe Nasini, painter of Siena, decorated the ceiling of the Venturini Chapel, where the Guido *Madonna* hung, with a fresco of St. Dominic ascending into heaven, carrying the Guido *Madonna* which he shows to the Trinity while wonderstruck angels look on. The inscription informs us that in 1221 Guido painted the picture and St. Dominic died; happy painter whose picture is shown to heaven just before the Saint ascends! The wording is as follows:

Guido de Senis hanc tabulam pingit, et D. Dominicus occumbit MCCXXI.
Felix pictor, cujus fortasse picturam Coelis ostendit, qui ea completa Coelis
ascendit.   (Bib. 80, ii, p. 638)

To the early eighteenth century it would certainly have seemed legitimate to romanticize upon the association; the inscribed date on the painting itself could be seen at any time and the death date of the Saint was of course well known. But while we find the fresco and its inscription no more than an amusing and naïve commentary, it may instead contain the explanation of the 1221 date on the Palazzo Pubblico *Madonna*.

On August 4 of 1221, at the height of his career, St. Dominic died after a short illness. His day and year of death are important in the calendar system of the Catholic Church. Thus, for instance, the great compilation of *Scriptores ordinis praedicatorum* (Bib. 140) begins on page 1 with:

1221. Sanctus Dominicus ordinis Fratrum Praedicatorum institutor . . .

In other words, the year 1221, since it represents the year of their founder's death, is *the* significant year in the Dominican Order.

The death of the Saint looms large in the events of 1221 but there are other reasons for the eminence of this date. On Whitsuntide (May 30) of 1221 the second General Chapter of the Dominican Order, presided over by Dominic himself, was held at Bologna. We know how busy he was in those times, both in Rome and Bologna, as well as in other cities. At some point or other, either in 1219 or 1220 or 1221, he stopped over in Siena, staying at the religious hostelry of Santa Maria Maddalena, located some ways out of the city. At the time a certain Imilia Malavolta, of the distinguished Sienese family, having retired from the world, was in charge of the hostelry. Perhaps at the time of Dominic's visit she turned over the monastery to him and to his Order. In any case, an *instrumentum donationis*, mentioned by early writers, is associated with the date of May 14, 1221 (Bib. 104). It is not inconceivable, then, to surmise that it was just at this time and in conjunction with this gift of a monastery that the Siena branch of the Dominican Order was established.

When we seek an explanation of the 1221 date on the Palazzo Pubblico *Madonna*, once in San Domenico, we would do well to inquire into the motivations of the monks who ordered the refurbishing of their *Madonna* at the beginning of the fourteenth century. Why should they order a modernization of practically the entire surface of the painting if they seriously intended to perpetuate the memory of Guido da Siena and his *Madonna*? And why associate painting and artist with a date fifty years earlier than the true one? The only possible answer is that the *Madonna* had by that time been designated to serve a commemorative purpose, not commemorative of Guido or of his *Madonna* but of the Dominican Order itself. Such an association between paintings and dates extrinsic to them is not so unusual in that period of historical inaccuracy. Other cases in point are the association of the San Bernardino *Madonna*

with the founding of a Franciscan Order (see Cat. No. V) and the supposed connection between the *Madonna del Voto* and the Battle of Montaperti (Cat. No. X).

At the beginning of the fourteenth century the Dominicans would still have known
by documents or legends that their Order had been established in Siena in 1221, the
very year of St. Dominic's death. To preserve this information for posterity and at
the same time to give their *Madonna* an enhanced venerability, must have seemed to
them a legitimate procedure. Such a falsification apparently gave no offense either
to the ecclesiastical authorities or to the laity but it has considerably bedeviled later
generations of critics.

BIBLIOGRAPHY

1442/3 Tura (in Garrison, Bib. 75), pp. 52-57.

1528 Tizio (in Brandi, Bib. 20), p. 103.

1625 Chigi (in Bacci, Bib. 9), p. 322.

c. 1625 Mancini, Bib. 105, pp. 66, 68, 166-67.

1649 Ugurgieri, Bib. 185, I, pp. 653-54; II, p. 329.

1702 Montfaucon, Bib. 123, pp. 350-51.

1716 Carapelli (in Milanesi, Bib. 120), p. 5.

1716 Gigli, Bib. 79, pp. 13, 27.

1723 Gigli, Bib. 80 (in 2nd ed., 1854), I, pp. 84, 86; II, p. 638.

pre-1733 Benvoglienti (in Della Valle, Bib. 56), pp. 238, 251, 254-55.

1770 Richard, Bib. 142, III, pp. 315, 317.

1782 Della Valle, Bib. 56, pp. 237-56.

1791 Montfaucon, Bib. 124, Pl. III.

1792 Lanzi, Bib. 94 (ed. 1815-16), I, pp. 11, 302-4.

1812 Da Morrona, Bib. 50, pp. 145-47.

1823 Seroux d'Agincourt, Bib. 154, II, pp. 100-1; III, pp. 127-28.

1827 Rumohr, Bib. 146, I, pp. 333-36; II, pp. 24, 165.

1839 Rosini, Bib. 144, I, pp. 130-33.

1840 Romagnoli, Bib. 143, p. 55.

1859 Milanesi, Bib. 120, pp. 4, 7, 8, passim.

1863 David, Bib. 52, pp. 107, 123.

1864 Crowe and Cavalcaselle, Bib. 46, I, pp. 181-85.

1885 Thode, Bib. 178, pp. 463-64.

1888 Strzygowski, Bib. 174, pp. 58, 147-49.

1889 Wickhoff, Bib. 198, pp. 244-55, 278, 285-86.

1890 Thode, Bib. 179, pp. 2-24.

1890 Thode, Bib. 180, pp. 25-28.

1895 Lisini, Bib. 96, p. 10.

1903 Douglas, Bib. 60, p. 160.

1903 Heywood and Olcott, Bib. 84, pp. 178-79, 208.

1906 Lusini, Bib. 103, pp. 263-64, 271-79.

1906 Davidsohn, Bib. 53, pp. 262-67.

1906 Zdekauer, Bib. 199, pp. 255-58.

1907 Venturi, Bib. 188, pp. 45-50, 52, 54.

1907 Jacobsen, Bib. 85, pp. 9, 17-20.

1907 Davidsohn, Bib. 54, p. 383.

1911 Weigelt, Bib. 191, pp. 211-22, 227.

1911 DeNicola, Bib. 58, pp. 433-35.

1911 Lusini, Bib. 101, pp. 65, 66, 69, 70, 143-44.

1912 Lusini, Bib. 102, pp. 63-65.

1912 DeNicola, Bib. 57, p. 5.

1915 Dami, Bib. 49, p. 114.

1915 Sirén, Bib. 169, p. 278.

1916 Sirén, Bib. 168, p. 7.

1919 Harvard, Bib. 81, p. 93.

1920 Berenson, Bib. 16, pp. 261-62.

1920 Marle, Bib. 110, p. 266.

1922 Weigelt, Bib. 192, pp. 280-84.

1923 Marle, Bib. 107, I, pp. 364-66.

1927 Toesca, Bib. 182, pp. 993-94, 1038 n. 44.

1928 Cecchi, Bib. 31, p. 172.

1928 Weigelt, Bib. 195, pp. 203-8.

1930 Weigelt, Bib. 194, pp. 2, 65 n. 11.

1931 Weigelt, Bib. 193, pp. 15-22.

1931 Brandi, Bib. 22, pp. 77-80.

1932 Berenson, Bib. 15, p. 269.

1932 Edgell, Bib. 61, pp. 26-35, 69, 70, 289.

1933 Siena, Bib. 164, pp. 23-24.

1933 Bacci, Bib. 11, pp. 5, 16-19.

1933 Brandi, Bib. 21, pp. 3, 11, 12, 13.

1934 Sandberg-Vavalà, Bib. 151, pp. 254-71.

1935 D'Ancona, Bib. 51, p. 87.

1937 Meiss, Bib. 115, p. 18.

1941 Coletti, Bib. 35, p. 28.

1943 Salmi, Bib. 147, p. 301.

1943 *Giottesca*, Bib. 167, p. 89.
1944 Coor, Bib. 41, p. 131.
1946 Carli, Bib. 26, pp. 23-24.
1947 Coor, Bib. 42, pp. 121, 123.
1948 Longhi, Bib. 100, p. 35.
1949 Coor, Bib. 38, pp. 13-14.
1949 Garrison, Bib. 73, pp. 109, 116 (No. 297).
1949 Sandberg-Vavalà, Bib. 152, p. 115.
1950 Offner, Bib. 133, pp. 61-90.
1951 Brandi, Bib. 23, pp. 248-60.

1951 Brandi, Bib. 20, pp. 94-124.
1953 Oertel, Bib. 129, pp. 42-43.
1953 Sandberg-Vavalà, Bib. 153, pp. 23-25, 38-40.
1954 Shorr, Bib. 155, pp. 8-9.
1955 Carli, Bib. 27, pp. 20-33.
1955 Carli, Bib. 29, pp. 176-78.
1955 Carli, Bib. 28, pp. 16-21.
1957 Stubblebine, Bib. 176, pp. 33-35.
1959 Stubblebine, Bib. 175, pp. 260-68.
1961 DeWald, Bib. 59, pp. 76, 77.

IVb. *Palazzo Pubblico Gable: Redeemer and Angels*

FIGURES 15, 68   Siena, Palazzo Pubblico   H 79 x W 180 cm.

The face of the Redeemer is in good condition, that of the angel on the right is in fair condition. The face of the angel on the left is completely repainted; it was not possible to remove the repaint during the recent cleaning inasmuch as the original face had been scraped away. There are a number of breaks due to subsurface disturbances.

The history of the panel is given under Cat. No. IVa.

This panel is from the hand of Guido.

This representation of the half-length Christ holding the Book in his left hand and blessing with his right recalls the Byzantine Pantocrator, and this is true even of the physical type. But, whereas that image represents Christ in Judgment, the same cannot be said for the theme in Guido's pediment. Rather, it should be related to similar groupings of Redeemer and angels, shown half-length, in the *cimase* of a number of painted crosses of the thirteenth century which, for the most part, belong to the circle of Bonaventura Berlinghieri. Such an arrangement is to be found in the Crucifix in Tereglio (Fig. 82). See also the examples in Garrison, Nos. 499, 500, 507, 508. Two examples of early Sienese crosses, in Montalcino and San Giovanni d'Asso, also have in their *cimase* a bust-length Christ flanked by angels (Bib. 149, figs. 156, 411). In all these cases the theme would seem to be the Ascension, shown in abbreviated form. According to Sandberg-Vavalà (Bib. 149, pp. 171, 190-92), the Ascension is the exclusive subject of the *cimase* in twelfth and thirteenth century crosses. Often it is presented as a full scene with the Virgin, Apostles, and angels beneath the figure or bust of Christ. Just as often the essential elements are abstracted from the Ascension, to be presented in lieu of it and symbolizing it. In the ambient of Bonaventura Berlinghieri the *cimasa* contains only the half-length figures of Christ and two angels. Given the fact that Guido's Altarpiece was the most ambitious such program of the time with little to guide the painter, we can imagine his turning to the programs of the large, impressive crosses which were produced in great numbers in the thirteenth century. If, as we believe, the gable of the San Domenico Altarpiece represents an abbreviated Ascension, it provides a suitable thematic climax, unifying the whole program of the Altarpiece, just as it does in painted crucifixes.

Critics have often given the opinion that the gable was added to the Palazzo Pubblico *Madonna* much later in the century, much later, that is, than the 1221 date which they still retain for the Madonna panel (Brandi, Bib. 23), an objection which is overcome when we date the *Madonna* late in the century. And in any case, the fracture on the left side of the gable, which is in line with the fracture on the left of the *Madonna*, is good evidence that the *Madonna* and the gable were originally painted on the same panel, suffered the same strains, and were only later hewn apart. The stylistic similarities between the figures in the gable and the other parts of the Altarpiece confirm the contemporaneity of the two parts. The right angel of the gable is a larger version of those in the spandrels while the hands and drapery patterns of the Redeemer correspond to those of the Virgin below. The identical forms and techniques of the haloes certainly betray a single creative moment.

IVc. *Badia Ardenga Narratives: The Infancy and Passion of Christ*
FIGURES 18, 20-30

Episode	Location	Size of Panel H. and W. in cm.
1. ANNUNCIATION	Princeton Museum	36 x 47
2. NATIVITY	Strolin Collection, Paris	36 x 47
3. ADORATION OF THE MAGI	Altenburg Museum	34 x 46
4. PRESENTATION IN THE TEMPLE	Strolin Collection, Paris	34 x 46
5. FLIGHT INTO EGYPT	Altenburg Museum	34 x 46
6. MASSACRE OF THE INNOCENTS	Siena Pinacoteca	32 x 37
7. BETRAYAL	Siena Pinacoteca	33.3 x 29.5
8. FLAGELLATION	Altenburg Museum	34 x 46
9. MOUNTING OF THE CROSS	Utrecht Museum	35 x 46
10. CRUCIFIXION	Siena Pinacoteca	33 x 45
11. DEPOSITION	Siena Pinacoteca	33 x 44
12. ENTOMBMENT	Siena Pinacoteca	33.5 x 44

These scenes were dispersed in the nineteenth century from the Badia Ardenga, a small abbey near Murlo, south of Siena. The five panels in the Siena Pinacoteca are mentioned in the 1852 catalogue (Bib. 157). An earlier manuscript catalogue of the gallery gives the information that they were deposited in the Pinacoteca in August of 1843 (Bib. 7). Three other panels were purchased for the Altenburg Museum in 1850 (Bib. 2). They were described at that time as parts of an altar-work, other parts of which J. A. Ramboux of Cologne had purchased. M. Ramboux had himself purchased three scenes as we know from the listing in the sale catalogue of his collection (Bib. 36). Two of these, the *Nativity* and the *Presentation in the Temple*, were later in the hands of the Munich dealer, Boehler, before they went to the collection of Strolin in Lausanne, and thence to the collection of his son in Paris. The third, the *Mounting of the Cross*, mistakenly called the *Crucifixion* in the Ramboux catalogue, ended up in the Archiepiscopal collection of the Centraal Museum of Utrecht (Bib. 186). Ramboux states that all his purchases were made in Italy during two periods: 1818-22 and 1832-42. We imagine that he must have purchased the Guido panels towards the end of the second period. The Princeton *Annunciation* was purchased in 1924 by the Princeton University Museum from the collection of A. L. Frothingham, who had bought it in Italy sometime earlier.

In recapitulation, five of the panels were in the Siena Pinacoteca by 1843, three went to Altenburg in 1850, and Ramboux had presumably purchased three by 1842. The panels were evidently still in the Badia Ardenga in 1834; in an inventory of that year certain paintings which have been reasonably identified with our group are mentioned as being in the rectory there: ". . . vari quadri assai usi nella canonica" (quoted by Brandi, Bib. 21). It is logical to suppose that these panels were put up for sale sometime between 1834 and 1842.

A clue to the earlier history of these narratives is contained in another document. In 1575 Monsignor Bossio, on a visit to Siena, describes an altarpiece he saw in the Badia Ardenga which was painted with scenes from the Passion of Christ:

> . . . altare unicum in dicta ecclesia existens . . . iconam depictam in tabula cum Passione D.N. Iesu Xri decenter factam.
>
> (quoted by Brandi, Bib. 22)

Bacci (Bib. 11) believes this is not a reference to our group of scenes because of the use of the word *icona*, suggesting a central image, but as Brandi (Bib. 21) points out, Bossio uses the team generically for every sort of altarpiece. It is likely that the narratives were in the Badia Ardenga in 1575 and that Bossio was referring to them in this entry in his manuscript.

If it is to be supposed that these scenes had come from San Domenico in Siena, the transfer must have taken place in the preceding half-century. In the 1520's Tizio, in his *History of Siena*, after his description of the *Madonna* in the Capacci Chapel, had gone on to mention that the wings which had formerly closed over the *Madonna* were hanging on the walls in another part of the same church (quoted above under Cat. IVa). We know from this that the *Madonna* and the narratives were separated; they probably had been so for a considerable time. When they were banished from the church, they were evidently sent to the Badia Ardenga to be fashioned into a sort of secondhand altarpiece, the *icona* which Bossio saw in 1575 and the *vari quadri* of the 1834 inventory.

IVc-1. *Annunciation*

FIGURE 18   Princeton, New Jersey, University Art Museum

The condition is generally good despite the fracture on the left side, which runs through the head of the angel, and the addition of strips of wood on the bottom and right sides. The gold in the upper left corner is of later date as are the sphere atop the cupola on the left and the roof of the leftmost building.

The scene is from the hand of Guido.

Most striking in this representation of the Annunciation is the posture of the Virgin, turning away from the Angel Gabriel as though in great fear, a pose which has been called the Shrinking Virgin motif (Bib. 115). It appears in several works of the 1270's such as the Spoletan Altarpiece in Antwerp (Garrison No. 360) and the predella of the Coppesque *Madonna* in Santa Maria Maggiore, Florence (Marle, 1, fig. 138). Most significantly we also find it in the mosaic in the Florence Baptistery (Fig. 84) which despite the absence of the formal characteristics of Cimabue's style may well reflect his design as do other scenes in the Baptistery decoration, suggesting his supervisory position there during the 1260's and 1270's. It is not hard to imagine that the motif of the Shrinking Virgin originated with Cimabue.

The Princeton *Annunciation* is perhaps the finest scene in the entire Badia Ardenga group. The Virgin, frozen yet tremulous in front of her tower, is in contrast to Gabriel whose forward propulsion is emphasized not only by his body but by his wings and draperies, and by the bending "dahlia" tree of the background. The complex harmonies of gold striations in the draperies of both figures register something of the emotional climate in this scene. The architecture, too, dramatizes the space and action: diminutive to the left, it looms large behind the Virgin.

BIBLIOGRAPHY

1925 Mather, Bib. 114, pp. 145-46.   1949 Garrison, Bib. 73, No. 687.
1937 Meiss, Bib. 115, p. 18.   1953 Sandberg-Vavalà, Bib. 153, p. 51.
1938 Oertel, Bib. 131, p. 266.   1959 Stubblebine, Bib. 175, pp. 260-68.

IVc-2. *Nativity*

FIGURE 20   Paris, the Strolin Collection

The surface of this panel is in good condition.
This scene is from the hand of Guido.

This scene is a faithful recitation of the Byzantine formula. The angels encircling the hillock-cave, especially the leftmost one and the one second from the right, are identical in feature and personality to the spandrel angels (Fig. 17) of the Palazzo Pubblico *Madonna*. Also similar to the latter is the face of the Virgin. The cave is modeled by distinct patterns of white highlights which give hardness and definition to the rock itself. No one in Guido's shop had anything like the master's command in such matters, as we can see by comparing the cave with that in the *Nativity* of the St. Peter Altarpiece (Fig. 53). Nor did any of them have that command of line found in the rippling gold hemline of the Virgin's mantle.

It is interesting that Crowe and Cavalcaselle, as early as 1864, could say of this scene that "its execution and style recall that of the angels in the San Domenico altar work by Guido."

BIBLIOGRAPHY

1864 Crowe and Cavalcaselle, Bib. 46, 1, p. 184 n. 3.
1867 Cologne, Bib. 36, p. 7.
1888 Cologne, Bib. 37, p. 131 n.

1931 Weigelt, Bib. 193, pp. 15-22.
1949 Garrison, Bib. 73, No. 671.
1959 Stubblebine, Bib. 175, pp. 260-68.

IVc-3. *Adoration of the Magi*

FIGURE 21   Altenburg, Germany, the Lindenau Museum

The condition is generally good. There are horizontal breaks at knee level and near the mountain top. The tree towards the right is a later addition.

This scene is from the hand of Guido.

Guido's *Adoration of the Magi* has an illustrious source, Nicola Pisano's Pulpit in the Siena Cathedral (Fig. 87). The similarities between the two works are numerous: the Christ Child already holding one of the gifts, the eldest magus kneeling and kissing the Child's foot, the curious motif of the crown placed over the arm of the kneeling magus, the two magi who in varying degree reveal the contents of their treasure, and the positions of the open-mouthed horses, one pawing the ground and another lowering his head as though to feed.

Weigelt (Bib. 191) noticed this relationship but because he believed that Guido worked in the first half of the thirteenth century, drew the conclusion that Nicola's Pulpit of the 1260's was based on Guido's version. Meiss (Bib. 117) restored this relationship to its proper sequence. The impressive influence of Nicola's Pulpit on Sienese painting is revealed once again, three decades later, in Duccio's *Maestà*.

As in the *Raising of Lazarus* (Fig. 13) in the Lenten Hanging of a decade earlier, the side of the building is shown diagonally. But in the *Adoration* the thin black and white lines of definition on the side of the building recede in a downward course. In the earlier work, these lines ran off in an upward course, dissipating the cubic density of the mass. It should also be noted that we are shown the side of the Virgin's throne as well and that there is an aperture at the bottom between the rear leg and the inverted bell flower which serves as a forward leg. This should help us to visualize the chair-throne of the Palazzo Pubblico *Madonna*.

BIBLIOGRAPHY

1898 Altenburg, Bib. 2, pp. 7-8.
1911 Weigelt, Bib. 191, pp. 232-35.
1916 Millet, Bib. 121, p. 151.
1931 Weigelt, Bib. 193, pp. 15-22.
1949 Garrison, Bib. 73, No. 660.

1951 Meiss, Bib. 117, pp. 101-102.
1952 Altenburg, Bib. 3, pp. 40-41.
1959 Stubblebine, Bib. 175, pp. 260-68.
1961 Oertel, Bib. 128, p. 57.

IVc-4. *Presentation of the Christ Child in the Temple*

FIGURE 23   Paris, the Strolin Collection

The condition is generally good. There are horizontal breaks at knee level and through the tower and baldacchino.

This scene is from the hand of Guido.

This scene is close to the *Presentation in the Temple* in the mosaic program of the Florence Baptistery (Fig. 85). Besides the grouping and the baldacchino, the similarity extends to the great mane of the priest and to his draperies made more ample by the bending posture. Although the mosaic is probably from a part of the decoration contemporary to Guido, it is not one of those where the style of Cimabue is seen. While there may be a connection between Guido's rendering and that in the Baptistery, both follow a Byzantine tradition.

In this centralized composition every form and action dramatizes the transfer of the Child from Simeon to the Virgin. The use of flanking architectural elements to delimit the space is typical of Guido's late narrative style.

BIBLIOGRAPHY

1867 Cologne, Bib. 36, p. 7.
1931 Weigelt, Bib. 193, pp. 15-22.

1949 Garrison, Bib. 73, No. 672.
1959 Stubblebine, Bib. 175, pp. 260-68.

IVc-5. *Flight into Egypt*

FIGURE 22   Altenburg, Germany, the Lindenau Museum

There is a horizontal break across the surface at the level of the Virgin's mouth. There is some repainting; the trees at the right and near Christ are later.

This scene is by Guido except for the landscape rocks which are by an assistant.

The composition is close to that in the mosaic of the Florence Baptistery (Fig. 85) but its rhythmic composition is very different from the static quality of the mosaic. The lively interplay of forms reminds us of Byzantine miniatures. Here, as elsewhere in the Badia Ardenga scenes, Guido's style has much in common with such scenes as those in the *Menalogium* of Basil II.

Nothing interrupts the left to right movement of the composition until the servant turns to glance at the Virgin and Child, a device which heightens the intense mood of the scene. The composition achieves considerable depth through the overlapping of the rock formations. The central figures are beautifully isolated between the hills and against the gold ground.

BIBLIOGRAPHY

1898   Altenburg, Bib. 2, p. 8.
1931   Weigelt, Bib. 193, pp. 15-22.
1949   Garrison, Bib. 73, No. 661.

1952   Altenburg, Bib. 3, pp. 40-41.
1959   Stubblebine, Bib. 175, pp. 260-68.
1961   Oertel, Bib. 128, pp. 57-58, 65.

IVc-6. *Massacre of the Innocents*

FIGURE 24   Siena Pinacoteca No. 9

The scene has been cut down by 7 cm. on the left side. Most of the surface is badly damaged. There is a horizontal break across the upper part of the panel.

This scene is by an assistant working on Guido's design.

The composition is remarkably close to that of the same scene in the Florence Baptistery (Fig. 86). In the mosaic Herod occupies a similar *aedicula* while the other figures mass to the left. In both scenes a soldier runs his sword through an infant held by the heels. Although it is possible that Guido was influenced by the Florentine work, it is well to remember that these two representations simply repeat a long-formulated Byzantine composition.

BIBLIOGRAPHY

1852   Siena, Bib. 157, p. 16.
1864   Siena, Bib. 158, p. 8.
1931   Weigelt, Bib. 193, pp. 15-22.
1932   Berenson, Bib. 15, p. 269.
1933   Bacci, Bib. 11, p. 18.

1939   Bacci, Bib. 7, p. 23.
1949   Garrison, Bib. 73, No. 696.
1958   Siena, Bib. 165, p. 19.
1959   Stubblebine, Bib. 175, pp. 260-68.

IVc-7. *Betrayal*

FIGURE 25   Siena Pinacoteca No. 10

This scene has lost 14.5 cm. from its left side. Parts of the remaining surface have been badly damaged, especially the faces of Christ and Judas.

Guido seems to have executed only the figures of Christ and the man with the club at the right.

Once again, the scene is close to that in the Baptistery in Florence (Fig. 86) and, as well, to the fresco version in the upper church at Assisi by a follower of Cimabue (Marle, I, fig. 270). Certainly the Guidesque scheme is closer to those than it is to that of Coppo di Marcovaldo in his San Gimignano Cross (Fig. 88).

Very probably the left side of Guido's picture contained a balancing architectural repoussoir. Christ extends his arm in front of Judas to effect the healing of Malchus whose figure at the left has been lost. The stocky man with the club seizes Christ by the shoulder; massed spears and lanterns compound the sense of confusion and violence.

BIBLIOGRAPHY

1852   Siena, Bib. 157, p. 16.
1864   Siena, Bib. 158, p. 8.
1929   Sandberg-Vavalà, Bib. 149, p. 425.
1931   Weigelt, Bib. 193, pp. 15-22.
1932   Berenson, Bib. 15, p. 269.

1939   Bacci, Bib. 7, p. 23.
1949   Garrison, Bib. 73, No. 697.
1958   Siena, Bib. 165, p. 19.
1959   Stubblebine, Bib. 175, pp. 260-68.

IVc-8. *Flagellation*

FIGURE 27   Altenburg, Germany, the Lindenau Museum

The condition is generally good except for the scratches on the head of the left-hand flagellant and repainting of his right arm and hand. Probably the panel was originally a rectangle and the unpainted upper right corner was cut off later.

This scene is from the hand of Guido.

A motif which is peculiarly Sienese has been pointed out by Meiss (Bib. 117); one flagellant holds a whip while the other holds a bundle of canes. The motif appears in the scene of the Flagellation in Duccio's *Maestà* and that by Ugolino in Berlin, as well as the *Flagellation* from the school of Duccio in the Frick Collection, New York. In Guido's scene the left-hand flagellant holds the canes in one hand while preparing to strike Christ with the flat of his other hand.

Once again, the lateral buildings bound the stage of action while the low-running architectural element unifies the scene. The disparity in the size of the two lateral buildings and its importance for understanding the altarpiece reconstruction is discussed below.

The Flagellation is frequently represented on historiated crosses but in no case do we find the same dramatic intensity and monumental composition. Admirable too are the portrayal of endurance in suffering and such fine details as the heaving old man at the right. The scene has a virile, tragic quality very different from the lyrical sadness of Duccio's scene.

BIBLIOGRAPHY

1898 Altenburg, Bib. 2, p. 8.
1916 Millet, Bib. 121, p. 635 n. 3.
1931 Weigelt, Bib. 193, pp. 15-22.
1933 Beenken, Bib. 14, p. 132.
1949 Garrison, Bib. 73, No. 662.

1951 Meiss, Bib. 117, pp. 98, 100.
1952 Altenburg, Bib. 3, pp. 40-42.
1958 Siena, Bib. 165, p. 19.
1959 Stubblebine, Bib. 175, pp. 260-68.
1961 Oertel, Bib. 128, pp. 58-59.

IVc-9. *Mounting of the Cross*

FIGURE 26   Utrecht, Centraal Museum, Archiepiscopal Collection

The condition is generally good although there are scattered damages at waist level.

The figures of the Virgin and Christ are by Guido; the rest of the scene is by an assistant working on Guido's design.

The scene of the Mounting of the Cross is rare in Italian painting. The representation in the Wellesley tabernacle center (Fig. 59) is a copy of the Guidesque scene by a follower. The scene also occurs in a panel from the school of Duccio in the Lee collection, Richmond (illustrated in *Diana: rassegna d'arte e vita senese*, VI, 1931, p. 58, plate 2-f), which is also so close to Guido's scene that it must be derived from it. In addition a Florentine Altarpiece in Berlin (Fig. 91) borrows this episode as well as several other ideas from Guido's Altarpiece. The only Tuscan example of a Mounting of the Cross definitely earlier than Guido's is that in Coppo's San Gimignano Crucifix (Fig. 88) where, however, the Virgin is absent and Christ does not mount the cross with any of the fervency found in Guido's scene.

The notion put forward many years ago by Montault (Bib. 122) that the Virgin is in the act of covering the naked thighs of Christ, a theory followed by van Marle (Bib. 107), is not very sensible. She definitely struggles to hold him back. Moreover, that the source for this representation is not St. Bonaventure is indicated by the fact that in the *Lignum Vitae*, the Saint describes how Christ was nailed to the cross while it was still on the ground (Bib. 19, pp. 77-78).

The intense drama revolves around the attempt of the Virgin to restrain her Son who so willingly approaches the cross while at the same time, she must fight off the youth at the left. The nails for the crucifixion, like the dark crosses, stand out ominously against the gold ground. With his sense for intervals, in his pattern of gestures, and with the facial expressions and lively draperies, as in the folds surging over the figure of the Virgin, Guido creates a tense and spirited drama.

BIBLIOGRAPHY

1867 Cologne, Bib. 36, p. 7.
1888 Jansen, Bib. 86, pp. 281-86.
1889 Montault, Bib. 122, pp. 84-85.
1889 Jansen, Bib. 87, p. 85.
1916 Millet, Bib. 121, p. 387.
1923 Marle, Bib. 107, 1, pp. 373, 379.
1923 Marle, Bib. 108, pp. 562-63.
1929 Sandberg-Vavalà, Bib. 149, pp. 278ff.

1931 Weigelt, Bib. 193, pp. 15-22.
1932 Berenson, Bib. 15, p. 269.
1933 Utrecht, Bib. 186, pp. 27-28.
1949 Garrison, Bib. 73, No. 702.
1951 Meiss, Bib. 117, p. 129.
1959 Stubblebine, Bib. 175, pp. 260-68.
1960 Meiss, Bib. 116, p. 18.

IVc-10. *Crucifixion*

FIGURE 28   Siena Pinacoteca No. 11

There are scattered surface damages due largely to the compound, horizontal break at waist level.

The Christ figure is by Guido; the rest of the scene is by an assistant working on Guido's design.

It is curious to see how little inspired Guido was by the interpretation of the Crucifixion scene on the Siena Cathedral Pulpit by the Pisani (Fig. 110); such elements as the swooning Virgin, the stricken Evangelist with his back to her, the crossed legs of Christ, and the Y-shaped cross had no effect on the painter. On the other hand, the formula of Cimabue's *Crucifixion* (Fig. 89) in the left transept of the upper church at Assisi influenced him overwhelmingly. The figure of the dead Christ has the same swing of the pelvis, nod of the head, position of legs and feet, and *perizoma* falling to a knotted point. The formula is also found in the Cimabuesque Cross in the Uffizi (*Giottesca*, fig. 83a).

The similarity continues in the grouping of the Virgin and the Evangelist together left of the cross, as well as in such particulars as the placing of the Virgin's right hand in the right hand of the Evangelist and her left hand against her breast. Curiously, Guido covers the Virgin's extended right hand with drapery, probably not for ritualistic reasons but to avoid the difficulty of representing interlocked hands. Likewise, he does not leave her left hand idle, as in the expressive gesture of Cimabue's figure, but has it clutch a fold of drapery.

The analogies continue on the right side of the scene. In both, the centurion sways back with one leg turned toward the right, his left hand holding his mantle at the waist, his head tilted, and his right arm flung up. Even the handling of the sleeve is similar. Likewise, both scenes have a lad in a short tunic peering out from behind the centurion, one leg planted firmly to the right, the shield pressed to his body with both hands, his left shoulder raised.

While the composition reflects the groupings of Cimabue's scene and detailed analogies can be made, everything has been simplified, as would indeed be necessary in so small a scale. There is little room for doubt that Guido borrowed all these elements from Cimabue, as has been pointed out previously by Millet (Bib. 121), Coor (Bib. 41), and Offner (Bib. 133). Unless a faithful replica of the Assisi fresco existed, it must be supposed that Guido had been in Assisi himself.

BIBLIOGRAPHY

1864 Siena, Bib. 158, p. 9.
1916 Millet, Bib. 121, p. 412 n. 7.
1929 Sandberg-Vavalà, Bib. 149, p. 55 nn. 42, 43; p. 808.
1931 Weigelt, Bib. 193, pp. 15-22.
1932 Berenson, Bib. 15, p. 269.
1933 Bacci, Bib. 11, p. 19.

1939 Bacci, Bib. 7, p. 23.
1944 Coor, Bib. 41, pp. 145, 149.
1949 Garrison, Bib. 73, No. 698.
1950 Offner, Bib. 133, p. 80 n. 12.
1953 Sandberg-Vavalà, Bib. 153, pp. 42, 45.
1958 Siena, Bib. 165, p. 19.
1959 Stubblebine, Bib. 175, pp. 260-68.

IVc-11. *Deposition*

FIGURE 29   Siena Pinacoteca No. 12

The damages and repainting to which this scene has been subjected are very great. The surface on the left has come away. There is much repainting in the figures. The tree on the right is a later addition. There is a horizontal break across the middle of the scene.

This scene is entirely by assistants on Guido's design. The principal figures of the Virgin, Christ, St. John, and Joseph of Arimathea are by the assistant who painted the Virgin, St. John, and the centurion in the *Crucifixion*.

For the greater part, Guido follows a rather unvarying Dugento formula, as may be seen by comparing it to the representation of the Deposition in the Crucifix by Salerno di Coppo in Pistoia (Bib. 149, fig. 249); see also the circle of Bonaventura Berlinghieri and the St. Francis Master (Bib. 149, figs. 245, 248).

There was probably a building on the left similar to that on the right, providing architectural brackets to the scene as in the *Crucifixion*. The curved body of Christ is held at the waist by Joseph of Arimathea while Nicodemus wrenches the nails from the feet. The most unusual feature of this representation is the way the Virgin stands on the second rung of the ladder so as to be at the proper height for holding the shoulders of her dead Son. This motif inspired the Florentine painter of the Altarpiece in Berlin (Fig. 91) who also borrows the scene of the Mounting of the Cross.

Duccio's quite similar *Deposition* in the *Maestà* differs chiefly in its sweetness and naturalness. In Guido's painting, the head and halo of Joseph of Arimathea intersect the two parts of the cross, an austere formality of a sort which Duccio carefully eschewed but which gives Guido's scene a great deal of solemn power.

BIBLIOGRAPHY

1864   Siena, Bib. 158, p. 9.
1916   Millet, Bib. 121, p. 481.
1929   Sandberg-Vavalà, Bib. 149, p. 452.
1931   Weigelt, Bib. 193, pp. 15-22.
1932   Berenson, Bib. 15, p. 269.

1939   Bacci, Bib. 7, p. 23.
1949   Garrison, Bib. 73, No. 699.
1953   Sandberg-Vavalà, Bib. 153, p. 42.
1958   Siena, Bib. 165, p. 19.
1959   Stubblebine, Bib. 175, pp. 260-68.

IVc-12. *Entombment*

FIGURE 30   Siena Pinacoteca No. 13

The panel is much damaged and repainted. The two cypresses are later additions, the one to the right hiding the third bloom of the "dahlia" tree. There is a horizontal break across the middle of the scene.

This scene is entirely by assistants on the design of Guido. There appears to be the same division of hands as in the *Deposition*: Christ, the Virgin, St. John, and Joseph of Arimathea are by the principal assistant of the *Crucifixion*.

The composition differs little from the formula in such a painted Crucifix as that by Coppo di Marcovaldo in San Gimignano (Fig. 88).

Although this scene was painted by assistants and although the composition is much confused by the addition of the two unattractive trees, a number of admirable things can be found in Guido's design. The hill on the left initiates a movement to the right through the bending tree to the hill at the right while the repeated curves of the figures rhythmically return the movement to the left and the head of Christ.

As much as anything in the Badia Ardenga scenes, the remarkable three-dimensionality of the sarcophagus demonstrates Guido's grasp of the new pictorial ideas. Coppo seems very remote now; Guido, having absorbed the lesson of Cimabue, is just a step from Duccio.

BIBLIOGRAPHY

1864   Siena, Bib. 158, p. 9.
1916   Millet, Bib. 121, pp. 503-4, 505, 515.
1923   Marle, Bib. 107, I, p. 373.
1929   Sandberg-Vavalà, Bib. 149, p. 464.
1931   Weigelt, Bib. 193, pp. 15-22.

1932   Berenson, Bib. 15, p. 269.
1939   Bacci, Bib. 7, p. 23.
1949   Garrison, Bib. 73, No. 700.
1958   Siena, Bib. 165, p. 19.
1959   Stubblebine, Bib. 175, pp. 260-68.

Reconstruction of the Altarpiece

FIGURE 16

The rectangular Palazzo Pubblico Madonna panel, by itself, without a gable, would be an anomalous shape for a Madonna Enthroned picture in the latter part of the thirteenth century and most critics have not hesitated to believe the gable was painted for it at the same time. Not only does the gable correspond in its dimensions and in at least one major fracture line, but the style is identical with that in the original parts of the panel below. Yet the two pieces, the *Madonna* and the pediment, are really not complete either; the frames, which are indubitably original, separate them in a way which has no parallel in Italian painting and, aesthetically, such a top-heavy work needs something more. Analogies with other altarpieces tell us this could have been furnished by lateral extensions in the form of narrative panels. There is a good deal of evidence to support the reconstruction of such an altarpiece with the Badia Ardenga scenes forming the lateral parts (Fig. 16). The problem was examined by this author in detail in 1959 (Bib. 175).

The twelve panels from the Badia Ardenga in their physical condition and in their measurements offer important clues. To begin with, the series of twelve panels forms two physically complete sections. This is borne out by the horizontal breaks in a number of the scenes. Where these fracture lines continue at a corresponding height in two flanking scenes, the inference is that the two scenes were painted on the same panel and the various stresses came through to the surface before the scenes were hewn apart. Thus, in the *Adoration*, the fracture just below knee level continues its slightly upward course clear across the *Presentation in the Temple*. The conclusion must be that the *Adoration* and the *Presentation in the Temple* were adjacent to one another and that the *Adoration* was to the left of the other scene. Comparable subsurface disturbances permit us to make comparable pairings of panels, so that we can place the *Massacre of the Innocents* after the *Flight into Egypt*, the *Flagellation* after the *Betrayal*, and the *Entombment* after the *Deposition*.

The reconstruction made by Weigelt (Bib. 193) in 1931 was faulty because he interspersed additional scenes into the Passion cycle, such as the Washing of the Feet, the Last Supper, and so on. In reconstructing Guido's cycle, he looked too much at the ample schedule in Duccio's *Maestà* and not enough at the programs on painted crosses which must have influenced Guido. A study of these reveals a terse accounting of the events of the Passion. For example, Coppo's San Gimignano Crucifix (Fig. 88) contains the scenes of the Betrayal, the Flagellation, Christ before the Judges, the Mounting of the Cross, and the Entombment. This is a familiar pattern of episodes for the Dugento, as can be seen from a glance at extant crucifixes with scenes in the side fields (see Sandberg-Vavalà, Bib. 149; also Garrison, pp. 199-203).

In addition, there is evidence offered in a Tabernacle in Perugia (Fig. 90) by an

Umbrian artist of the latter part of the thirteenth century. The Madonna is set under a cusped arch in a gabled panel, which is already enough to suggest a connection with Guido, as we shall see subsequently. This central image is flanked by narratives in an abbreviated program which, nevertheless, is helpful for reconstructing Guido's scheme. Even Weigelt, aware of its relevance, did not explore the possibilities sufficiently. For example, the *Entry into Jerusalem* in the Perugia Tabernacle closes the cycle of the Mission of Christ and is the last scene on the left shutter. Weigelt, however, places it at the beginning of the Passion in his reconstruction of Guido's Altarpiece, again, presumably, following the program of Duccio's very different *Maestà*. The Passion in the Perugia shutter begins, therefore, in the same swift and decisive way we noticed in Coppo's Crucifix, with the *Betrayal* and the *Flagellation*. The evidence is strong that Guido's program began similarly.

A principal clue to the correct ordering of the scenes in Guido's Altarpiece is the irregular shape of the Flagellation scene (Fig. 27) with its cut-off upper right corner. As Beenken (Bib. 14) pointed out, the cut corner of the *Flagellation* must have some reference to the original shape of the work to which it belonged. The diagonal termination of the scene can be decided from the composition itself: the low buildings on the right, the high ones on the left, and the rhythmic movement of the figures and the story inward and upward. The same is true, in reverse, of the scene occupying the corresponding position on the opposite side of the Altarpiece, the *Annunciation* (Fig. 18). Here the composition moves in toward the right, and the tower of the Virgin is far larger than the diminutive architectural elements on the left. And here, the upper left corner, in an area equal to that cut from the *Flagellation*, has been filled in with small architectural embellishments and a gold ground. It would appear that after the scenes had been taken apart, the corner of the *Annunciation* was painted in, whereas the corner of the *Flagellation* was cut off. The conclusion is inescapable that both scenes were composed with the irregularity of shape in mind, as the subtle compositional adjustments indicate.

The measurements of the individual scene, as near as can be judged through the different painted borders of later date, were just about 44 cm. across by 33 cm. high. The aggregate height of the six extant scenes on either side, with their original, thin painted borders, is equal to just half the available space on either side of the Palazzo Pubblico *Madonna* when the diagonal frame of the gable is extended downward. Such an enframement would also account for the irregular corners of the *Annunciation* and the *Flagellation*; when the scenes were placed in their respective cycles, the descending line of the frame would have cut off the upper left angle of the *Annunciation* and the upper right angle of the *Flagellation*. We can therefore hypothesize two additional groups of six scenes each for the lower part of the Altarpiece.

Guido's narrative program undoubtedly embraced the cycle of Christ's Infancy, that of his Teaching or Mission, the Passion, and the cycle of the Resurrection, a recital which is covered in twenty-four episodes. It should be possible to reconstruct the missing parts with such a program in mind. Weigelt's reconstruction of the two cycles for the lower part, the Mission and the Resurrection, is excessive and his selection doubtful. The Mission probably began with the Christ Child Teaching in the Temple, a rare subject in the Dugento but one which appears in the Perugia Tabernacle (Fig. 90). In Guido's swift-paced narrative this would have been followed by the Baptism and then the Temptation. When Weigelt included all three Temptations of Christ, he was evidently influenced by the expansive narrative scheme of Duccio's *Maestà*. The Perugia Tabernacle has only the first Temptation, and Guido's cycle probably had the same. Then would have followed the important representation of the Transfiguration, seldom omitted from the cycle. The last two scenes would have been the Raising of Lazarus and the Entry into Jerusalem. We have already seen that Guido would not have placed the Entry in the Passion cycle, preferring to begin that group with the Betrayal.

The Resurrection cycle probably began with the Three Marys at the Tomb, an episode which appears with the greatest frequency in the thirteenth century. The Descent into Limbo also has ample precedent in the period. The Noli Me Tangere, which also appears in the Perugia Tabernacle and which is a familiar Dugento theme, would come next. The scene beside it may well have been another landscape episode, the Way to Emmaus, a popular episode on the historiated crosses of the time. The last two scenes in the group would have been the Supper at Emmaus and the Pentecost. Both these scenes appear with great frequency. The Supper at Emmaus, usually a symmetrical composition with architectural elements, would serve to balance in these respects the traditional rendering of the Pentecost. It would also compensate for the absence of the Last Supper in the Passion cycle, similar in iconographic content as it is. The Pentecost appears in the Perugia Tabernacle. The chief omission from this sequence of scenes is, of course, the all-important Ascension. But this, as we have seen, is alluded to in the gable above the central *Madonna*, where, in the abbreviated form of a half-length Christ and two angels, it is similar to the representations in the *cimase* of painted crosses. It is significant that the scene never appears in the apron of a painted cross, but is reserved for the *cimasa* where it serves as a climax of the drama unfolded beneath.

If all these parts are put together, the resultant shape would be a gabled panel similar to Bonaventura Berlinghieri's 1235 *St. Francis* in Pescia (Fig. 62), but more complex in the use of moldings between the various sections. Certainly the gabled panel was a popular form in the thirteenth century (see Garrison, Group XXII). A basic difficulty with Weigelt's interpretation is that he clings to Tizio's idea of "wings," implying a tabernacle with shutters that close over the central area. Weigelt's rectangular wings have no aesthetic, architectonic relation to the pedimented central part. We would expect the wings either to cover the pediment when closed or else to fit under the cusped arch of the Madonna panel (see Garrison, Groups IX, XI-XV). This would have been unwieldy in so large a size. The Perugia example cited above is unusually large for a tabernacle, having a height of 215 cm.; the Palazzo Pubblico *Madonna* with its gable is 362 cm., an unimaginable height for a tabernacle. Besides, the diagonal cuts on the *Annunciation* and the *Flagellation* rule out such an arrangement. Were the diagonal lines of the Palazzo Pubblico gable extended down to cut off the corners of the *Annunciation* and the *Flagellation*, we would expect the angles formed above the two scenes to equal the corner angles of the two scenes. Now the isosceles triangle of the pediment has angles of 100, 40, and 40 degrees. Although it is difficult to control the measurement of the angle formed by the diagonal within the two scenes, it is not more than a degree or two off. It is significant that the narrative fields as here reconstructed fit within the areas controlled by the descending diagonals of the frame. Allowing a few centimeters for narrow, painted borders between scenes and a molding between upper and lower cycles, everything fits quite closely.

The Guido Altarpiece must have had the most elaborate system of framing and inner moldings yet seen in Siena (Fig. 15). The module for all the moldings and the framing is established by the width and design of the cusped arch. It is 5.3 cm. wide and is a band raised on its outer edge and bisected by a molding which is ridged on its inner side. The border around the Madonna panel consists of two such moldings, separated by a flat band, also 5.3 cm. wide which, as Offner (Bib. 133) has pointed out, was originally painted a dark blue, similar to the band in the Polyptych No. 7 (Fig. 7). The inner gold molding, then, served as a border for the Madonna while the outer one edged the inner side of the narrative fields.

The triangular spaces above the narratives may have been filled in one of several ways. A company of angels would complement those in the spandrels above the Madonna and those in the pediment. But knowing Guido and the Sienese we can imagine those spaces filled with some sort of decorative scrolls and, possibly, medallions, in a similar system to that employed in the large spaces of his Polyptych No. 7.

It has been suggested by Coor (Bib. 39) and Oertel (Bib. 128) that the twelve scenes would constitute a complete program if they were crowned by a Resurrection theme. This is unlikely. For one thing, there is no example of a crucifix with narratives which does not include some elements from the Resurrection cycle besides the abbreviated Ascension which invariably appears in the *cimasa* of the cross. In almost every known instance there is at the very least a representation of the Three Marys at the Tomb. And in paintings with a Madonna rather than a representation of the Crucified in the center, it is equally true. Even a Tabernacle in Assisi (Garrison No. 325) with an abbreviated schedule of scenes which jumps from the Adoration to the Betrayal includes the Three Marys at the Tomb. The large Tabernacle in Perugia discussed above as having affinities to Guido's work contains four scenes from the Resurrection cycle: the Three Marys, the Noli Me Tangere, the Ascension, and the Pentecost.

Oertel (Bib. 128) reconstructs a low, gabled dossal with the twelve Badia Ardenga scenes flanking a small Madonna or a representation of the Salvador Mundi. This reconstruction is largely premised on his doubt that the Badia Ardenga scenes could have belonged with the Palazzo Pubblico *Madonna* because there are no comparable examples of such large altarpieces preserved from the time. It is significant that in Tizio's time the two "wings" he saw were still associated with the Palazzo Pubblico *Madonna*. Such reports are usually based more on fact than fiction and nowadays we are beginning to give them more credence than formerly. The panels Tizio saw, although not wings, were apparently large enough to constitute side panels for the impressively large *Madonna* or he would not have said so. To him, they looked as though they would fit and could, as he says, "close over the *Madonna*." They must also have appeared to belong to the *Madonna* on stylistic grounds, that is, recognizably Dugentesque in style.

Tizio's statement is in itself proof that a pair of wings large enough for the Palazzo Pubblico *Madonna* existed in San Domenico, even if the Badia Ardenga scenes are not to be identified as partial remains of them. If Oertel's reconstruction is to be believed, we must presume a lost central panel equal to the height of three of the scenes, that is, just half the available space under the Palazzo Pubblico frame, as well as a gable of ample enough proportions to encompass all that would have been contained beneath. Further, we would have lost the pair of shutters Tizio saw which were of a size to fit the Palazzo Pubblico *Madonna*. All these lost sections would have had to have been painted by Guido and in the 1280's. All such parts, having measurements in a ratio to the Palazzo Pubblico *Madonna*, lead us to believe that the only lost panels are those containing the other twelve narrative scenes of our reconstruction.

To say that the Palazzo Pubblico *Madonna* and the Badia Ardenga narratives cannot have belonged together in a large altarpiece for the reason that comparable paintings are not to be found at the time is to ignore the great size and complex programs of painted crosses which, as we have seen, inspired parts of Guido's program. Furthermore, it is quite likely there may have been other, earlier altarpieces containing a Madonna and scenes, which have been lost. As an example, the Pistoiese Fioravanti, writing at the beginning of the seventeenth century, mentions a large *Madonna* on the high altar of San Zeno in Pistoia, signed by Coppo di Marcovaldo and dated 1275, which he says was surrounded by delightful narrative scenes: "una Madonna con il Bambino in collo, grande, con vaga storietta a torno . . ." (Bib. 8). Coor (Bib. 45) rejected the idea that the Madonna could have been flanked by narratives because no comparable examples can be found from this time. What is clear and pertinent and not to be rejected quickly is that Fioravanti, who, as Bacci (Bib. 6) points out, is reliable, specifies that there was such a large *Madonna* with scenes. Although Coor is correct in rejecting the measurements of eight braccia high by four braccia wide, given in a later, inaccurate chronicle, it was apparently a work of substantial proportions which Coppo painted in 1275.

One must also bear in mind the multiple repercussions of the San Domenico Altarpiece found in later thirteenth century paintings, repercussions which could only have been occasioned by the impressive Altarpiece which Guido's must have been. The evidence of the Perugia Tabernacle (Fig. 90) is important. To begin with, it is itself a very large representation of a Madonna Enthroned and it is flanked by double rows of narratives. These are from all four cycles of the Christ story and many of them parallel the Guidesque selection. The Madonna panel itself is gabled and the central figure is placed under a cusped arch; this combination is not otherwise found outside the Guido ambient and at once suggests an influence from that source.

The Berlin Altarpiece (Fig. 91), from the Florentine school of the end of the century, likewise may have been inspired by Guido's Altarpiece. Here, too, a central Enthroned Madonna is flanked by a summary selection of Passion scenes which includes a representation of the Mounting of the Cross, derived from Guido's scene. Also, the Deposition scene of the Berlin panel borrows the motif invented by Guido, the Virgin standing on the second rung of the ladder. Finally, the Berlin picture is a gabled panel very close in shape to Guido's Altarpiece. Whereas the painter of the Perugia work recast his Guidesque borrowings into the older tabernacle format, the painter of the Berlin work maintained the gabled shape of the San Domenico Altarpiece. Only in this light can we understand the otherwise unique combination of an Enthroned Madonna and narratives in a gabled panel. That no other example of this combination is known in thirteenth century painting heightens the belief that the unoriginal painter of the Berlin panel was, in this work, dependent upon the innovations of a more progressive artist.

Both the Berlin and Perugia pictures are simplified and have more summary selections of scenes, yet both in their various ways, give evidence of an influence from some more important work than theirs essayed to be, Guido's San Domenico Altarpiece.

Reflections of this important Altarpiece are found in other places. The *Mounting of the Cross* was imitated a number of times, not only by Guido's shop, but by other Sienese and Florentine painters. The basic compositions of several episodes were repeated in the St. Peter Altarpiece (Fig. 53) of a few years later. The Madonna panel itself was copied in the Galli-Dunn version (Fig. 43) during the same decade, and was still deemed a worthy prototype at the end of the century when the San Gimignano *Madonna* (Fig. 60) was made. The most important influence of all, of course, was that exerted on Duccio. If hindsight be permissible, it seems doubtful that his *Maestà* of a little over two decades later, with its great Madonna and surrounding full program of narratives, could have been an entirely new thing under the sun. History does not work that way. As such matters evolve, it is reasonable to believe that some sort of precedent existed for Duccio, neither more nor less complex and evolved than the San Domenico Altarpiece.

BIBLIOGRAPHY

1528 Tizio (in Brandi, Bib. 20), p. 80.
1575 Bossio (in Brandi, Bib. 22), pp. 102-3.
pre-1852 Milanesi (in Bacci, Bib. 7), p. 23.
1852 Siena, Bib. 157, p. 16.
1859 Milanesi, Bib. 120, p. 4.
1864 Crowe and Cavalcaselle, Bib. 46, I, pp. 181 n. 1, 184 n. 3.
1867 Cologne, Bib. 36, pp. 1, 7.
1890 Thode, Bib. 179, p. 7.
1895 Siena, Bib. 160, pp. 6-7.
1898 Altenburg, Bib. 2, p. 8.
1903 Siena, Bib. 161, pp. 6-7.
1907 Jacobsen, Bib. 85, pp. 11-12.
1911 Weigelt, Bib. 191, pp. 226-27.
1920 Marle, Bib. 110, p. 269.
1922 Weigelt, Bib. 192, p. 280.
1923 Marle, Bib. 107, I, p. 373.
1929 Sandberg-Vavalà, Bib. 149, pp. 55, 394, 425, 452, 464, 808.
1931 Brandi, Bib. 22, pp. 77-80.
1931 Weigelt, Bib. 193, pp. 15-22.
1932 Bacci, Bib. 10, pp. 189-95.

1933 Brandi, Bib. 21, pp. 12-13.
1933 Bacci, Bib. 11, pp. 16-18.
1933 Utrecht, Bib. 186, pp. 27-28.
1933 Beenken, Bib. 14, p. 132.
1933 Siena, Bib. 164, pp. 108-110.
1937 Meiss, Bib. 115, p. 18.
1939 Bacci, Bib. 7, pp. 21-28.
1949 Garrison, Bib. 73, pp. 116, 125.
1950 Offner, Bib. 133, pp. 60, 80 n. 12.
1951 Brandi, Bib. 23, p. 255.
1951 Brandi, Bib. 20, pp. 118-19.
1953 Coor, Bib. 43, pp. 257-58.
1953 Sandberg-Vavalà, Bib. 153, pp. 23, 40-46.
1954 Coor, Bib. 39, pp. 82-83.
1955 Carli, Bib. 27, p. 29.
1955 Carli, Bib. 28, p. 10, 28.
1958 Siena, Bib. 165, p. 19.
1959 Stubblebine, Bib. 175, pp. 260-68.
1961 DeWald, Bib. 59, pp. 79-80.
1961 Oertel, Bib. 128, pp. 57-67.

ASSISTANTS–DECADE OF THE 1270's

V. *San Bernardino Madonna*

FIGURE 31   Siena Pinacoteca No. 16   H 140 x W 97 cm.

The lower part of the panel was cut off, probably in the seventeenth century; the loss includes the lower part of the throne and the legs of the Madonna. Perhaps at that time the gable was recut to an arch shape, although this might have been done during an earlier refurbishing of the panel. It was filled out to a gable shape once again in the 1931 restoration. At that time repaint was removed from the Madonna's mantle. The surface is rubbed and damaged, especially in the left cheek of the Madonna and the angels in the medallions. Long, vertical cracks are present to the left and right of the halo of the Madonna. The stones are missing from the haloes.

The inscription, now lost, but notarized in the seventeenth century, is said to have run as follows:

ISTA · TABULA · E · FRATERNITATIS · BEATE MARIAE · SEMPER · VIRGINIS · QUA
FECIT · FIERI · IN · A·D·M·C·C·L·X·I·I·

(This panel is [the property] of the Fraternity of the Blessed Mary ever Virgin, they having had it made in A.D. 1262.)

The painting was originally in the Church of the Compagnia di Santa Maria degli Angeli in Siena. The name of the church was later changed to San Bernardino in honor of that local saint. At the suppression of the lay fraternities in 1783 this painting went into the collection of the Abate G. Ciaccheri who later gave it to the Biblioteca Comunale. It went to the Pinacoteca of Siena in 1816.

Most of the discussion of this panel has depended on the assumed veracity of the inscription. Since a 1262 date does not seem plausible on stylistic grounds, as shall be seen, the history of the inscription must be scrutinized.

Padre Della Valle in his *Lettere senesi* of 1782 describes the painting and mentions a document which he saw in the books of the Company testifying to the inscription and the 1262 date. His comment follows a discussion of the *Madonna del Voto*, the venerable age of which he has just supported by a quotation from the 1442 chronicle of Ventura. Through a printer's error the quotation marks continue for several pages, giving the impression that it is Ventura and not Della Valle who discusses the San Bernardino *Madonna*; this has also been noted by Garrison (Bib. 77). Cesare Brandi (Bib. 21) rediscovered the document in the Archivio di Stato, Siena. In 1655 Franciscus Johannis Baptistae de Panichis, *notarius publicus ac civis senensis*, was called in by the Company to prepare a statement certifying that the inscription at the foot of the Madonna had undergone considerable disintegration. To preserve the memory of it from oblivion, the Company requests him to make a transcript of it from memory which he does, word for word:

> . . . quod propter antiquitatem temporis memoria infrascripta et scripta in pede Immaginis Beatissimae Virginis . . . cepit devastari; ob id ne remaneat de caetero improbata antiquitas picturae ipsius Beatissimae Virginis et ne in oblivionem ipsa probatum ex memoria reducatur, et ut veniat ad perennem memoriam Posterorum . . . ipsi venerabiles Confrates mandaverunt et rogaverunt me Notarium infrascriptum ut in presenti pagina de dicta memoria et dicto originali conficerem exemplum prout ita fecit, et est sequentis tenoris . . .

He proceeds to give the inscription, "verbo ad verbum nihilo addito vel diminuto . . ."

The rediscovery of this document has convinced most critics of the reliability of the inscription and its date. But several questions may be asked. How long before the notary public was called in did the mutilation of the panel take place? Was it simply a matter of weeks, months, or rather within the living memory of those who decided on the notarization? It is curious that Ugurgieri, so diligent in such matters, does not mention the inscription when he writes of the panel six years earlier; it must have been illegible or cut off by that date. One hesitates to impugn either the Fraternity or the notary public and prefers to believe that the time interval was not too great. But if it is probable that the 1262 date actually existed on the painting in the seventeenth century, it is not certain that such an inscription with such a date had been there from the time the panel was painted.

The year 1262, as we know, is the year in which a group of Franciscans, probably tertiaries, founded the Compagnia di Santa Maria degli Angeli (Lusini, Bib. 101). That the Company would have ordered a painting for the altar in the very year of the founding and presumably before an edifice could have been erected does not seem very plausible. A more attractive theory is that the Company may in an early period have had an inscription added, which in the seventeenth century was assumed to be contemporary with the completion of the painting. Possibly in the early fourteenth century, when the Palazzo Pubblico *Madonna* underwent modernization and was given a back-dated inscription, the Company of Santa Maria degli Angeli might also have wished their *Madonna* to be doubly venerated by the addition of an early date. More likely, though, the motivation was the same as in the case of the Palazzo Pubblico *Madonna*, where a similar inscription commemorated not the painting or the painter but the origin of the particular religious order in Siena. Indeed, the very wording of the inscription sounds more like a property claim than an artist's inscription. The 1655 notarization may be accurate in what it reports, but the inscription it reports may not be coeval with the rest of the painting. If the style of the picture indicates some date earlier or later than 1262, it would seem better to discount the inscription as evidence. It is well to remember, finally, that the two inscriptions on Guidesque Enthroned Madonnas are, to say the least, suspicious. Probably there was no tradition in the shop for inscriptions on such panels. In thirteenth century painting, in fact, only about nine Madonnas Enthroned bear an inscription (Bib. 42, pp. 120, 123 and Bib. 76, p. 53).

In its entirety the San Bernardino *Madonna* surely represented a full-length, enthroned Madonna and Child of the type common in the Guido shop. Along with the Arezzo and Florence *Madonnas* (Figs. 32, 39), it represents the earlier Guidesque formula which prevailed in the 1270's, the decade before the Palazzo Pubblico *Madonna* and its successors. The Arezzo panel may be an imitation of the San Bernardino painting but it is possible that all the *Madonnas* in this group are based on a lost prototype by Guido himself, in which the master, largely abandoning the schemes of Coppo di Marcovaldo, was in the process of absorbing the impressive inventions of Cimabue. For this development of the Madonna Enthroned, and the place of the San Bernardino *Madonna*, see the Arezzo *Madonna* (Cat. No. VI). To believe that Guido or, for that matter, an assistant could have arrived at such a formula as early as 1262, a date we no longer believe has anything to do with the painting, and which is only one year later than the date of Coppo's Siena *Madonna* (Fig. 80), is to misconstrue the pace of developments in Dugento painting.

For those critics who have abandoned the 1221 date for the Palazzo Pubblico *Madonna*, the San Bernardino *Madonna* has generally been cited as the first work by Guido (e.g., Bib. 45), but we can accept neither the 1262 date nor the authorship of Guido himself.

While this panel is of high artistic merit, as may be seen in the coherent rhythm of striations in the draperies, in the convincing modeling of forms and in the vivacity of expression on the face of the Madonna (Fig. 92), it reveals none of the touch of Guido himself. The Madonna's head is more square than oval and unusually plastic, her right hand has none of the claw-fingered elegance of, say, the hands in the Polyptych No. 7 by Guido (Fig. 8). Indeed, the pronounced volumetric qualities of this work only point up the fact that Guido's approach to forms is essentially a linear one. The San Bernardino Master ranks high among the Guidesque painters, though little of his work remains to prove his skill. A probable attribution to his hand is the half-length *Madonna* in Princeton (Fig. 42).

BIBLIOGRAPHY
(for additional bibliography see *Giottesca*, Bib. 167, p. 89)

1649 Ugurgieri, Bib. 185, pp. 654-55.

1655 Panichi (in Brandi, Bib. 21), p. 10.

1716 Gigli, Bib. 79, p. 27.

1752 Pecci, Bib. 137, pp. 111-12.

1782 Della Valle, Bib. 56, pp. 239-41, 251, 275-76.

1792 Lanzi, Bib. 94 (ed. 1815-16), I, p. 304.

1816 De Angelis, Bib. 55, p. 13.

1842	Siena, Bib. 156, p. 1.		1933	Brandi, Bib. 21, pp. 3-13.
1852	Siena, Bib. 157, p. 5.		1933	Siena, Bib. 164, pp. 116-18.
1864	Crowe and Cavalcaselle, Bib. 46, pp. 180-81.		1934	Sandberg-Vavalà, Bib. 151, pp. 259ff, 267-68.
1864	Siena, Bib. 158, p. 8.		1937	Salmi, Bib. 148, p. 350.
1895	Siena, Bib. 160, pp. 9-10.		1943	Giottesca, Bib. 167, p. 89.
1903	Douglas, Bib. 60, p. 161.		1946	Carli, Bib. 26, p. 26.
1903	Heywood and Olcott, Bib. 84, p. 320.		1946	Coor, Bib. 45, pp. 236-37.
1904	Rothes, Bib. 145, pp. 37f.		1947	Coor, Bib. 42, pp. 121, 123.
1907	Venturi, Bib. 188, pp. 50-52.		1949	Coor, Bib. 38, pp. 13-14.
1907	Jacobsen, Bib. 85, p. 17.		1949	Garrison, Bib. 73, No. 430.
1911	Weigelt, Bib. 191, p. 222.		1950	Offner, Bib. 133, p. 62.
1911	Lusini, Bib. 101, p. 143 n. 23.		1955	Carli, Bib. 27, pp. 20-22.
1914	Perkins, Bib. 138, p. 97 n. 1.		1955	Carli, Bib. 28, pp. 20ff.
1920	Marle, Bib. 110, p. 268.		1957	Stubblebine, Bib. 176, p. 33 n. 32.
1922	Weigelt, Bib. 192, p. 281.		1958	Siena, Bib. 165, p. 14.
1927	Toesca, Bib. 182, pp. 994, 1038 n. 44.		1960	Garrison, Bib. 77, pp. 23-24, 57-58.
1928	Weigelt, Bib. 195, pp. 203-8.		1961	DeWald, Bib. 59, p. 78.
1932	Berenson, Bib. 15, p. 269.			

VI. *Arezzo Madonna*

FIGURE 32   Arezzo Pinacoteca No. 2   H 198 x W 122 cm.

This panel, like the San Bernardino *Madonna*, was originally a gabled panel, and like that other painting, was reduced to the round-topped shape at a later time. The lower part of the panel is largely repainted: draperies, footstool, left side of the throne, legs of the Child, left hand of the Madonna. The upper part of the panel is in considerably better condition. On either side of the halo of the Madonna there is an inscription: MHP ΘΥ.

Salmi and Vita in their 1921 catalogues of the Arezzo Pinacoteca state that the panel came from the Church of San Francesco in Arezzo, as had Crowe and Cavalcaselle (1864). All identify it with the *Madonna* seen by Vasari in the Cappella della Concezione of San Francesco. Salmi suggests that it may have come from the Franciscan church at Poggio del Sole since the Franciscan church at Arezzo only dates from the early fourteenth century.

The principal value of the Arezzo panel lies in the light it throws on the original aspect of the San Bernardino panel and on the early Madonna Enthroned formula used in Guido's shop. Its throne, as we can see despite repaint, consists of a blocklike mass built up in a system of horizontal divisions of broad leaf-decorations separated by thin, richly decorated bands. This is, it will be recalled, the same style found in the throne of the *Virgin in Glory* by Cimabue (Fig. 95) in the upper church at Assisi and in the thrones in the four panels which reflect an early phase of Cimabue: the

Madonnas in the Acton collection, Florence (Fig. 96), the church of San Remigio, Florence (Fig. 97), the Galleria Sabauda, Turin (Fig. 98), and the church of Sant' Andrea, Mosciano (Fig. 99). As in the Arezzo panel, these Cimabuesque *Madonnas* have no finials decorating the forward corners of the throne seat, a feature which becomes important in the next phase as one more space marker.

Other early features of the Arezzo *Madonna* are the straight-backed posture of the Child, the white, softly waved headcloth of the Virgin, and the manner in which she holds the maphorium under the Child. These features are all found in the San Bernardino *Madonna* (Fig. 31) and, significantly, in Coppo's Siena *Madonna* (Fig. 80) of 1261. This confirms the notion of Coppo's influence on Guido and the relative earliness of the San Bernardino and Arezzo *Madonnas*.

The probable derivation of this panel from the San Bernardino *Madonna* in the Siena Pinacoteca or from a prototype which may have served them both is evident. Not only is the Arezzo panel less pleasing on the whole but in details it falls far short of the achievement in the painting from San Bernardino. For example, the decoration of the throneback, an exciting labyrinth of designs in the San Bernardino panel, is made up of fairly inorganic, aimless squiggles in the Arezzo painting. Where the gold striations on the drapery of the Madonna figure in the San Bernardino panel always suggest the presence of body forms beneath, the striations in the Arezzo panel run independent and aimless courses. Such comparisons can be multiplied, as in the differences between the veils and the way they fall to a point: so crisp in the Siena example, so uncertain in the Arezzo one. The conclusion seems inescapable that the painter of the Arezzo panel was a lesser member of the shop, capable only of copying a painting by the master or by another, more talented assistant. This is the only work we can trace to his hand. A date in the early 1270's close to the San Bernardino *Madonna* is reasonable.

BIBLIOGRAPHY

1568 Vasari, Bib. 187, p. 360.
1864 Crowe and Cavalcaselle, Bib. 46, p. 166.
1888 Strzygowski, Bib. 174, p. 150.
1890 Thode, Bib. 179, pp. 3, 4, 5.
1907 Venturi, Bib. 188, pp. 50, 52.
1911 Weigelt, Bib. 191, p. 213.
1914 Perkins, Bib. 138, p. 97 n. 1.
1915 Vita, Bib. 190, pp. 77-78.
1916 Sirén, Bib. 168, p. 8.
1920 Marle, Bib. 110, p. 268.
1921 Arezzo, Bib. 5, pp. 10-11.
1921 Arezzo, Bib. 4, p. 5.
1923 Marle, Bib. 107, I, pp. 285-86, 368.
1925 Falciai, Bib. 63, p. 55.

1927 Toesca, Bib. 182, I, p. 1034 n. 44.
1928 Weigelt, Bib. 195, pp. 203-8.
1930 Weigelt, Bib. 194, p. 63 n. 4.
1932 Berenson, Bib. 15, p. 268.
1934 Sandberg-Vavalà, Bib. 150, p. 41.
1934 Sandberg-Vavalà, Bib. 151, pp. 260, 268.
1948 Longhi, Bib. 100, p. 36.
1949 Coor, Bib. 38, pp. 13-14.
1949 Garrison, Bib. 73, No. 178.
1953 Sandberg-Vavalà, Bib. 153, pp. 27, 29, 30.
1955 Carli, Bib. 27, pp. 22, 23.
1955 Carli, Bib. 28, p. 22.
1957 Stubblebine, Bib. 176, p. 33 n. 32.

VII. *Polyptych: Madonna and Child with SS. Paul, Peter, John the Evangelist, and Andrew*

FIGURES 33, 41   Siena Pinacoteca No. 6   H 102 x W 214 cm.

This panel has been cut down on the ends with the consequent loss of a figure on either side; the edge of the one on the left can still be seen. Parts of the spandrel angels to the left and right have also been lost as well as most of the angel on the Madonna's left. The gold ground is much abraded but the figures are in good condition. The molding around the edge is original; the frame is modern.

That the panel has been in the Pinacoteca since at least the early nineteenth century is borne out by De Angelis who in 1816 describes a painting, No. 17 in the gallery at that time, as being similar to one by Vigoroso. The panel still bore the number 17 in the 1842 catalogue. The reference to Vigoroso has continued in all subsequent catalogues which list this work. Quite possibly this was one of the paintings which formed the nucleus of the Pinacoteca in the late eighteenth century.

This Polyptych is a variant of Guido's own Polyptych No. 7 (Fig. 7). The similarity is continued today by the coincidence of the loss in both panels of the lateral figures on each side. Despite a few differences, such as the inclusion of other saints, this panel follows the program and the format of the Polyptych No. 7 so that the work could easily be assigned to the shop.

A curious divergence from the No. 7 Polyptych is the omission of the Madonna's white headcloth. Instead, the Virgin's blue robe is drawn up, cowl-fashion, over the head. This formula is also found in the half-length *Madonna* in Princeton (Fig. 42) and in the *Madonna del Voto* (Fig. 37).

Despite this one late feature the Polyptych most probably dates from the same decade as the No. 7 Polyptych, which it imitates. Such close adherence to the style and composition of the master is characteristic of the shop work in the 1270's. In many ways the painter merely copies mechanically without any of the *brio* of the No. 7 Polyptych. The chief variation is the angels in the spandrels whose wings spread in such a way as to echo the rhythm of the arches. But we can hardly go along with Brandi (Bib. 22) in his high praise of this work. The figures seem disassociated from one another, partly the result of the curious disparity in scale. In such matters the painter is less than inspired and the contrast to the No. 7 panel by Guido is great.

This painting introduces us to an assistant who followed Guido's formula more scrupulously than most and who will be seen again several times. The similarities between this painting and the *Madonna del Voto* (Fig. 37) lead to the conclusion that the same hand was responsible for both. In the mantle of the Madonna in each case there is the same endless and almost aimless weaving of gold striations; similar too is the drawing of the hands in the representation of the Child and of the Madonna.

In both, the Madonna is wooden-faced, with a white line echoing the upper lip, the same vertical shadow dividing the nose from the farther cheek. The Child has the same wig of hair and square jowl. Both paintings have stamped ornament in the haloes. A number of these characteristics may be found in the *Madonna* in Florence (Fig. 39), which is also probably from the hand of this assistant whom we call the Madonna del Voto Master.

BIBLIOGRAPHY

1816 De Angelis, Bib. 55, p. 15.
1842 Siena, Bib. 156, p. 4.
1890 Thode, Bib. 179, p. 5.
1895 Siena, Bib. 160, p. 5.
1903 Siena, Bib. 161, p. 5.
1907 Venturi, Bib. 188, pp. 47, 50.
1907 Jacobsen, Bib. 85, p. 11.
1911 Weigelt, Bib. 191, p. 222.
1920 Marle, Bib. 110, pp. 268-69.
1922 Weigelt, Bib. 192, p. 281.
1923 Marle, Bib. 107, I, p. 372.
1931 Brandi, Bib. 22, p. 78.

1932 Berenson, Bib. 15, p. 269.
1932 Edgell, Bib. 61, p. 34.
1933 Brandi, Bib. 21, p. 11.
1933 Siena, Bib. 164, pp. 115-16.
1934 Sandberg-Vavalà, Bib. 151, pp. 260, 267, 268.
1949 Garrison, Bib. 73, No. 435.
1950 Offner, Bib. 133, pp. 62, 76.
1953 Sandberg-Vavalà, Bib. 153, pp. 23, 34, 35, 39.
1958 Siena, Bib. 165, p. 19.

VIII. *Lord and Virgin Enthroned*

FIGURE 34   Siena, Church of the Convent of the Clarisse   H 97 x W 59 cm.

The cleaning of 1947-48 removed repaint which had covered all but the faces. The gold ground and haloes are badly abraded. Areas now repainted are indicated by slanted lines: the platform, the lower left side, the left knee of the Lord, most of the book and the part of the throneback between the figures. Unrepainted damages are present in the face of the Virgin and in her headcloth. The roundel decoration in the border on either side and at the top has all but disappeared.

The panel has come into the literature only recently, following the cleaning of 1947-48.

Dugento representations of the Lord and Virgin Enthroned in a scene other than a depiction of her coronation are rare (see Cat. No. XIV). In the thirteenth century we find scenes comparable to ours in the choir of the upper church at Assisi by Cimabue (Fig. 95) and in the last scene on the St. John Altarpiece in the Siena Pinacoteca (Marle, I, fig. 215). Much earlier, ca. 1143, we find the *Lord and Virgin Enthroned* in a Roman mosaic in Santa Maria in Trastevere (Bib. 182, fig. 622). In the Roman example the Virgin is already crowned whereas the crown does not appear in the Tuscan examples. In all examples except the Clarisse panel there are other figures accompanying the principal ones; in Cimabue's fresco saints and angels surround the Virgin, who extends her right arm toward them while the Lord blesses them. In the St. John panel the Baptist is present, recommended by the Virgin to the Lord's blessing. In the earlier mosaic in Rome, the enthroned are flanked on either side by a row of saints and ecclesiastical authorities. Here too the Virgin acts as intercessor. The Clarisse panel is unusual, then, in the isolation of the two figures. There is no possibility of a lateral extension to include other figures in the same space since the wide border, originally decorated with a pattern of disks, clearly terminates the composition on either side.

More unusual is the fact that the Virgin is placed on the left hand of the Lord; generally she appears on his right hand, although exceptions can be found. It is possible that in this position the Virgin is intended to represent the Bride rather than the Mother of Christ.

The prototype for the Guidesque representation would logically seem to be the *Virgin in Glory* (Fig. 95) in Assisi by Cimabue. The period of Cimabue's Assisi work has been much disputed. It has been noted, however, that the Orsini arms are to be found in the Evangelist webs of the crossing vault in the upper church. On stylistic grounds these web decorations appear to be later than the representations in the choir and can be associated with the pontificate of an Orsini, Pope Nicholas III (1277-80). Cimabue's *Virgin in Glory*, therefore, is probably a work of the early or middle 1270's (Bib. 176, pp. 32-35).

That the Clarisse panel is not much later in date may be estimated also by the fact that Coppo di Marcovaldo seems to have exerted a strong influence on the painter; the energetic contrapposto of the figure of the Lord is reasonably close to that of Coppo's *Madonna* (Fig. 81) in Orvieto, which is probably of the late 1260's. This is especially to be noted in the lifted right leg and foot.

The most certain indication of the date emerges in relating this work to the others attributed to this assistant: the Memphis Polyptych (Fig. 50), the San Gimignano Crucifix (Fig. 55), and the Krakow Tabernacle (Fig. 56). The name of the Clarisse Master has been given to the painter of this oeuvre (Bib. 74, Bib. 73, and Bib. 133). The similarities observed are the curious carved quality of the forms, the shaping of the features, the incisive detailing of finger joints, and the patterns of gold striations on the draperies. From these comparisons a fairly coherent personality can be adduced. He adheres most closely to the Guidesque formula in this Clarisse panel; greater carefulness and tightness in drawing is exercised in the draperies and white headcloth and in the delineation of features here than in his other works. Although he refers to Coppo's Orvieto *Madonna* in his Krakow Tabernacle, the Coppesque reference seems more precise in the figure of the Lord in the Clarisse panel, with the emphatic contrapposto and the lifted knee. From all this it would seem likely that the Clarisse panel is to be dated in the 1270's when the painter was obedient to the disciplines of Guido and not too distant from the work of Coppo. For the subsequent development of this assistant, see Cat. Nos. XVII, XXI, and XXII.

BIBLIOGRAPHY

1947 Garrison, Bib. 74, p. 303 n. 13.   1950 Offner, Bib. 133, pp. 72-73 n. 8.
1949 Garrison, Bib. 73, p. 15 and No. 161.   1957 Coor, Bib. 40, p. 329 n. 12.

IX. *Gallerani Reliquary Shutters: St. Dominic Prays for the Cure of the Blessed Reginald Who Is Given a Dominican Habit by the Virgin, The Blessed Andrea Gallerani Praying before a Crucifix, Stigmatization of St. Francis, The Blessed Andrea Gallerani Distributing Alms.* EXTERIOR: *The Blessed Andrea Gallerani Receiving Beggars and Pilgrims*

FIGURES 35, 36   Siena Pinacoteca No. 5   H 121.5 x W 71 cm.

Each panel has a vertical split seen on the interior and exterior. There are some surface damages but the condition is generally good. The panels were originally reversed; the present right hand panel formed the left shutter and the left hand panel formed the right shutter.

There is an inscription on the exterior side, above the figure of Gallerani, which reads: · s̄ · ANDREAS.

Thode in 1885 and the Siena catalogue of 1864 list the Shutters as No. 17. In the 1852 catalogue they are listed as No. 13 while in the catalogue of 1842 they are No. 11. In 1816 De Angelis mentions "una specie di dittico" containing representations of several saints among whom he finds SS. Francis, Dominic, and Thomas Aquinas. Probably De Angelis confused the identity of the Blessed Andrea and St. Thomas. If so, we can trace the Shutters back to 1816.

Bacci (Bib. 7) cites the evidence of Monsignor Bossio who visited the church of San Domenico in 1575 and saw there the altar dedicated to the Blessed Andrea Gallerani. According to Bossio, there was an altar containing the remains of Gallerani and in front of it there was a grille, on either side of which were panels depicting his various miracles:

> Visitavit altare sub titulo B. Andreae Gallerani senensis . . . supra quod altare aderat icona imaginis Beati Andreae cum variis miraculis per eum factis in tabulis perpulcre et ornate depictis subtilissime. Cui icona aderat gratis ferrea et post illam aderat capsa lignea deaurata in qua erat repositum corpus supradicta B. Andreae.

Bacci is most probably correct in identifying the panels seen by Bossio with the No. 5 Shutters in the Pinacoteca.

From the Chronotaxis of A. M. Carapelli, 1716 (quoted in Bacci, Bib. 7), we know that the altar of Beato Gallerani was remodeled in 1685 and his bones were placed elsewhere, after which there are no further accounts of the panels mentioned by Bossio.

Gallerani was a tertiary Dominican which explains the locus of his cult. When the panels are reversed, the scene of St. Dominic Praying takes the place of honor in the upper left; this strengthens the assumption that these panels came from San Domenico and are identical with the ones Bossio saw in that church.

The cult of Beato Gallerani was a local one and the inscription " · s̄ · ANDREAS" was of popular origin since he was not canonized by the Church. He was chiefly revered for his charitable acts (he founded a hospital for the poor in Siena) and for his posthumous miracles. Particularly amusing is the story of how, to keep from dozing off during his prayers, he tied a cord around his neck, the other end affixed to a rafter, illustrated in the scene of Beato Gallerani Praying before a Crucifix. The life of Gallerani is contained in the *Acta Sanctorum* (Bib. 1). This is in turn based on the "Legenda beati Andree," a fourteenth century manuscript in the Biblioteca Comunale of Siena. There is also a seventeenth century life of the Blessed Andrea (Bib. 13).

As we have noted, a surprising number of critics do not distinguish qualitatively between the Reliquary Shutters No. 4 (Fig. 1) and the No. 5 pair. It is significant that Bacci assigns them both to one follower of Guido whom he refers to as the "Maestro del Beato Gallerani," thus imputing a certain preeminence to the No. 5 Shutters. Yet it is just in a comparison with the No. 4 Shutters by Guido that the inferior quality and also the later date of the No. 5 Shutters can be determined. In the *Stigmatization* (Fig. 100) of the No. 5 Shutters, the rocks have become doughy masses from which only the sparsest vegetation can grow. The tower lacks the gleaming accent of its complement in the No. 4 Shutters (Fig. 101), and its gateway has become an impassable niche. The Seraph is of inferior design and smothered in drab wings which offer the greatest contrast to those sharply defined, luminous feathers in the No. 4 scene. Curiously, the three rays descending from the Seraph to the Saint in Guido's scene have been omitted altogether here. It is noteworthy that the Seraph of the No. 4 *Stigmatization* establishes psychological contact with the Saint by gazing directly at him while in the No. 5 scene the glance of the Seraph wanders off. The pose of the St. Francis imitates that of the earlier work; that it is less successful may be due to the murky drapery deprived of those lustrous, schematic lines found in the draperies in the other scene. Throughout the scenes of the No. 5 Shutters we find that the drapery is treated in the simplest possible terms; the painter uses dark instead of white accents and these are generally devoid of decorative interest. We find none of the careful, linear etching of both contour and fold which distinguishes the work of Guido.

The quality of the figures can be judged by a comparison of the figure of the Crucified in the scene of Gallerani Praying (Fig. 102) with that in the Badia Ardenga *Crucifixion* (Fig. 103). Guidesque in posture and schematization, the figure in the No. 5 scene nonetheless has an elongated body and a disproportionately small head. Such weaknesses in drawing can be found in a number of places, notably the atrophied arm and hand of Gallerani in the scene of Gallerani Distributing Alms (Fig. 114). It should be noted that the four pilgrims on the exterior share three pairs of legs.

The figure of the Crucified in the No. 5 is helpful in dating the Shutters, as Bacci has pointed out. The posture of the figure and the draping of the *perizoma* are similar to those in the Badia Ardenga scene and to those of the Crucifix in Perugia by the St. Francis Master, dated 1272 (Marle, I, fig. 218). It does not seem likely that we would find this formula before the 1270's.

A further indication of the date of the Shutters is afforded by a glance at the early references to Gallerani. We do not know the date when Gallerani was beatified but it may have been soon after his death in 1251. The first indication of his status comes in 1274 when Bernard, the Bishop of Siena, granted an indulgence of a year for those who visited his tomb on Holy Monday (Bib. 7, pp. 18-19). A date in the mid 1270's would agree very well with such stylistic factors as the figure of the Crucified discussed above and with the style of the painting in general. It is logical to suppose that the reliquary arrangement described by Bossio may have been established at about this time, when the fame of Gallerani's miracles had spread and the indulgences were announced.

The stylistic similarities of these scenes to those in the St. Peter Altarpiece (discussed under Cat. No. XIX) strongly suggest that the Shutters were made by the same hand but at an earlier date. For a reconstruction of the oeuvre of the St. Peter Master, see Cat. Nos. XVI, XIX, and XX.

BIBLIOGRAPHY

1575 Bossio (in Bacci, Bib. 7), p. 7.
1816 De Angelis, Bib. 55, p. 12.
1842 Siena, Bib. 156, p. 3.
1852 Siena, Bib. 157, p. 7.
1864 Siena, Bib. 158, p. 9.
1885 Thode, Bib. 178, p. 150.
1895 Siena, Bib. 160, pp. 4-5.
1907 Jacobsen, Bib. 85, p. 10.
1907 Venturi, Bib. 188, v, p. 102.
1911 Weigelt, Bib. 191, pp. 216-18, 225.
1915 Sirén, Bib. 169, p. 278.
1916 Sirén, Bib. 168, p. 8.
1916 Millet, Bib. 121, p. 412 n. 8.

1922 Weigelt, Bib. 192, p. 282.
1923 Marle, Bib. 107, p. 372.
1928 Cecchi, Bib. 31, p. 15.
1929 Sandberg-Vavalà, Bib. 149, pp. 808, 870.
1931 Brandi, Bib. 22, p. 78.
1932 Berenson, Bib. 15, p. 269.
1933 Siena, Bib. 164, pp. 114-15.
1939 Bacci, Bib. 7, pp. 3-32.
1952 Kaftal, Bib. 90, pp. 53-57, 313.
1953 Sandberg-Vavalà, Bib. 153, p. 46.
1955 Carli, Bib. 28, p. 30.
1956 White, Bib. 197, pp. 344, 347.
1958 Siena, Bib. 165, pp. 17, 19.

ASSISTANTS–DECADE OF THE 1280's

X. *Madonna del Voto*

The surface is very scratched and rubbed. The removal of most of the votive jewelry has left the surface of the painting pocked with nail holes. The panel is greatly cut down on all sides; fragments of the original moldings remain in the two top corners.

The history of the painting has long confounded critics. Recently Garrison (Bib. 75, 78) exhaustively explored the documentary evidence surrounding the *Madonna*; this by and large supersedes previous discussions. The problem stems from the confusion between two *Madonnas* associated with the early history of the Siena Cathedral: the Guidesque *Madonna del Voto* and the *Madonna* now in the Opera del Duomo (Fig. 79) which is a fragment of a horizontal altarpiece. The matter is further confused by the three different names which have been associated with the Guidesque *Madonna;* in the fifteenth century the sources refer to it as the *Madonna delle Grazie* and once as the *Madonna degli occhi grossi*. From then on we find it being referred to as the *Madonna delle Grazie* until, in the nineteenth century, the title of *Madonna del Voto* gradually becomes common. The sources allow us to follow the history of the painting under one name or another as far back as the fifteenth century. Since that time it has been in its present location in a chapel of the Siena Cathedral which itself has successively borne the titles: Cappella di San Bonifacio, Cappella di Alessandro Settimo, Cappella delle Grazie, and finally Cappella del Voto, its present title.

According to our earliest sources of the fifteenth century the Guidesque *Madonna* had formerly been on the high altar of the Cathedral. This would mean that it had been removed from that position by at least 1311 when Duccio's *Maestà* was installed. While we have no contemporary documentation for this transfer, we can assume it was of sufficient interest to be remembered, either in records or by word of mouth, until the time of an inventory of 1423 or of Ventura's Account of the Battle of Montaperti of 1442, both of which state that the *Madonna* had previously been on the high altar of the Cathedral.

A principal clue to the original shape of the *Madonna del Voto* is supplied by the portions of the thin moldings still intact on the panel. A sufficient portion of the inner molding exists to make it quite certain that it was originally a cusped arch. This cusped molding fits very closely around the Virgin's head, her halo just fitting into the central foil. This precludes the possibility put forward by Lusini (Bib. 101) that the panel was originally a full-length, enthroned Madonna. Not only is the amplitude of space customary in such a representation lacking here, but the absence of the throneback found in all Guidesque examples of the Madonna Enthroned warns against any such interpretation. Moreover, the absence of the Virgin's head-cloth and of the maphorium under the Child, both standard elements in Guidesque representations of the Madonna Enthroned, also suggests a different iconographic scheme.

That the *Madonna* could have been part of a polyptych has been suggested by Garrison (Bib. 78). Several documents are of interest in relation to this theory. In 1448 and 1455 the authorities empowered the Operaio of the Cathedral to cut the *Madonna delle Grazie* to a smaller size so that it would have greater portability in processions. In one of the documents the painting is described as "magne latitudinis et magni ponderis." The suggestion of unwieldy width and heaviness leads us to imagine an original format of a rather long, low, gabled dossal following the Guidesque mode used in the Polyptychs Nos. 6 and 7 (see Fig. 9a). The Madonna would have been flanked by a series of half-length figures. In our reconstruction (Fig. 38) the Polyptych has been restored with two saints on either side. The usual polyptych of the thirteenth century has a five-figure composition; the two Guidesque examples with seven figures, Polyptychs Nos. 6 and 7, are exceptional and even these eventually lost their terminal figures. The only other Guidesque example, the Memphis Polyptych (Fig. 50) of the later 1280's, is also a five-figure composition. The argument for a reconstruction with five figures is strengthened when we realize that the large size of the *Madonna del Voto* (82 cm. in its present, fragmented state) is considerably larger than that of the Madonnas in the other polyptychs, so that a composition with seven figures would have made a prohibitively wide dossal.

When we analyze the thin, relief moldings of the *Madonna del Voto,* we discover that, besides the cusped arch, there are the remnants of additional moldings. These are apparently segments of two arched moldings which circumscribed the inner cusped arch. This set of triple moldings, although not found elsewhere in Guidesque works, does occur in later painting.

We have a number of clues for the restoration of the Madonna del Voto Polyptych to its original aspect. There is a good possibility that the 1301 Pisa Polyptych (Fig. 76) by Deodato Orlandi reflects fairly closely the original form of the Madonna del Voto Polyptych and serves as a reliable guide to its reconstruction. That Deodato, basically an eclectic, would have taken elements from the Madonna del Voto Polyptych is not difficult to believe, considering the esteemed position it must have enjoyed as the principal altarpiece in the Siena Cathedral. It should be noticed first of all that Deodato has borrowed the Guidesque polyptych form: a long, low-pitched, gabled panel. Using a system similar to that seen in the *Madonna del Voto,* Deodato enframes each figure by a cusped arch bounded in turn by a compound molding. While other Guidesque polyptychs have the cusped arch only over the central Madonna compartment, it had been used over all the figures in Meliore da Toscana's 1271 Polyptych (Fig. 74) and came into general favor later on, as in Simone Martini's Pisa Polyptych of 1320 (Fig. 78). We suspect the system may have been used in the Madonna del

Voto Polyptych, much as it was in Deodato's. Deodato may have taken other elements from the Guidesque Polyptych, such as the angels spread-winged in the spandrels. This motif, Sienese and Guidesque in origin, was already present in the Polyptych No. 6 (Fig. 33) and may in all likelihood have been used in the Madonna del Voto Polyptych.

Equally important is the presence of colonnettes in Deodato's Polyptych, which separate and clearly compartmentalize the figures. Originally of Florentine usage, they are seen in Cimabue's row of angels at Assisi (Fig. 77), in Meliore da Toscana's 1271 Polyptych (Fig. 74), and in other examples. Although they do not occur in earlier Guidesque works, it is not unlikely that they made their first appearance in Siena in the Madonna del Voto Polyptych; colonnettes appear reduced to a painted form in the San Gimignano *Madonna* (Fig. 60) and as thin, elongated, relief moldings in the St. Francis Altarpiece (Fig. 61). The system, which makes it far easier for the artist to fix his figures in a definable space, is used consistently from the end of the thirteenth century, as in the polyptychs of Duccio and then of Simone Martini.

The dating of the *Madonna del Voto* has usually been based on information in the early histories of Siena in which the *Madonna* was connected with the Battle of Montaperti of 1260. This battle was an important signpost in Sienese history, marking as it did the triumph of Siena over its rival Florence. Moreover, the victory was interpreted as a favor granted by the Virgin, whose cult was strong in Siena. When in 1442 Ventura wrote his account, based on still earlier versions (Bib. 75), he claimed that the *Madonna* now in the Opera del Duomo had been the *Madonna* on the high altar of the Cathedral to which the Sienese had offered their prayers before the battle. Ventura also believed that the *Madonna delle Grazie*, the present *Madonna del Voto*, was painted soon after the battle of 1260 in commemoration, replacing the older image on the high altar. Ventura's dating of the second *Madonna* was undoubtedly based on the Sienese tradition that the scroll held by the Christ Child signified the donation of Siena to the Virgin as a fiefdom. The scroll is, of course, merely a traditional element of iconography and originally had no relation to the donation of the city. But this association undoubtedly had great appeal to the popular imagination and thus what began as legend became established fact.

A more reliable guide to the dating of the *Madonna del Voto* is to be found in the molding scheme. The thin type of molding strip that is used here is not found in the Guidesque ambient until the Galli-Dunn *Madonna* (Fig. 43), the St. Peter Altarpiece (Fig. 53), and the Montaione *Madonna* (Fig. 54), works which date in the 1280's and later. Moreover, the triple set of moldings, so in advance of those of the earlier Polyptychs No. 7 (Fig. 7) and No. 6 (Fig. 33), as well as the inclusion of colonnettes, is conclusive evidence that the *Madonna del Voto* could not have been executed earlier than the middle of the 1280's.

The painting is very competent in quality, but no more than that. The artist adheres closely to all the standard shop devices. An analysis of its style indicates that it was probably painted by the assistant who made the Polyptych No. 6 (Fig. 41) and the Florence *Madonna* (Fig. 39). The face of the Madonna and her draperies differ in no significant detail from those features in his other works. Because of the pre-eminence of this work in his oeuvre, the designation, Madonna del Voto Master, seems just. For a further analysis of the style of this important assistant, see Cat. Nos. VII and XI.

It is probable that the design of the Madonna del Voto Polyptych is to be attributed to Guido himself. The invention of the more elaborate moldings, for example, bespeaks the creative powers of the master and not an assistant, no matter how faithful. This still leaves unanswered the question of why so important a commission as this, destined for the high altar of the Cathedral, was not executed by the master himself. It may have been due to the increased work in Guido's shop, now at the height of its productivity. Or, it is possible that Guido was dead by this time; we have no works from Guido's own hand after this time and the subsequent activity of the shop is marked by a gradual removal from a pure Guidesque style. This is, however, admittedly hypothetical. It is to be expected that if this painting were to have been executed by anyone in the shop other than Guido, it would be by this assistant, the one who most closely followed the style of his master.

BIBLIOGRAPHY

(for additional bibliography see Garrison, Bib. 78)

1423	Siena Cathedral Inventory (in Garrison, Bib. 78, pp. 15f.)	1911	Weigelt, Bib. 191, pp. 218, 221.
1442	Ventura (in Garrison, Bib. 75, p. 43, and Bib. 78, p. 16)	1911	De Nicola, Bib. 58, p. 435.
		1911	Lusini, Bib. 101, pp. 65, 66, 69.
1448	Siena (in Garrison, Bib. 78, p. 16)	1920	Marle, Bib. 110, p. 268.
1455	Siena (in Garrison, Bib. 78, p. 17)	1922	Weigelt, Bib. 192, p. 282.
1625	Chigi (in Bacci, Bib. 9, p. 298)	1923	Marle, Bib. 107, I, p. 368.
1716	Gigli, Bib. 79, pp. 5, 13, 27.	1928	Weigelt, Bib. 195, pp. 206, 207, 210.
1723	Gigli, Bib. 80 (in 2nd ed., 1854), II, p. 511.	1931	Brandi, Bib. 22, p. 78.
		1932	Berenson, Bib. 15, p. 269.
1752	Pecci, Bib. 137, pp. 2-3.	1933	Brandi, Bib. 21, pp. 3, 11.
1782	Della Valle, Bib. 56, pp. 222-27, 240.	1934	Sandberg-Vavalà, Bib. 151, p. 268.
1784	Faluschi, Bib. 64, p. 4.	1939	Lisini (in Muratori, Bib. 126, vol. xv, Part 6, 1939, p. 314 n. 1).
1792	Lanzi, Bib. 94 (ed. 1815-16), I, p. 301.		
1839	Rosini, Bib. 144, pp. 133, 137 n. 36.	1949	Garrison, Bib. 73, No. 650 and p. 74.
1840	Romagnoli, Bib. 143, pp. 7-8.	1950	Offner, Bib. 133, pp. 62, 65.
1859	Milanesi, Bib. 120, p. 93.	1951	Brandi, Bib. 20, pp. 117, 120-24.
1893	Lisini, Bib. 97, pp. 10-11.	1960	Garrison, Bib. 75, pp. 55-57.
1903	Heywood and Olcott, Bib. 84, p. 236.	1960	Garrison, Bib. 78, pp. 5-22.
		1961	DeWald, Bib. 59, pp. 78-79.

XI. *Florence Madonna*

FIGURE 39   Florence Academy No. 435   H 125 x W 73 cm.

A heavy vertical cleavage runs along the entire left side of the panel. There are scattered damages in the painted border, in the tunics of the Child and of the Madonna, in her hands, and in several parts of the throne. The oval stones are missing from both haloes. Except as noted, the surface is in good condition.

The painting came from the collection of Charles Murray, Florence, in 1889. It was in the Uffizi in 1907; Weigelt lists it as Uffizi No. 5 in 1922. It was moved to the Florence Academy and listed as No. 26 in the 1925 Academy catalogue, as No. 25 in the 1928 and 1932 catalogues, as No. 435 in the 1936 and 1951 catalogues.

Only Sandberg-Vavalà (Bib. 153) has given any attention to details which might locate this painting in Guido's milieu. Thus she correctly distinguishes a number of early and late features. Early features are the absence of a cusped arch, the vertical position of the Child, the left hand of the Madonna clutching the maphorium, and the abundance of material falling in zigzags from the left wrist of the Madonna. In all these features the Florence *Madonna* relates to the Arezzo and San Bernardino *Madonnas* (Figs. 32, 31). Certain other features, however, indicate a cognizance of the later Madonna Enthroned formula. The headcloth of the Madonna is now decorated with gold striations and it no longer falls to a point on the breast. The maphorium is arranged in a circular shape under the Child. The small colonnade on the lowest level of the throne and the finial on the left forward corner of the throne seat are features not found on the throne of the Arezzo panel; they appear in the throne of the Galli-Dunn *Madonna* (Fig. 43) and were present on the throne of the Palazzo Pubblico *Madonna* (Fig. 73). This type of decoration is also found in the fairly late St. Peter panel (Fig. 53) and, much elaborated, in the Rucellai *Madonna* (Fig. 125) by Duccio. Most advanced of all is the throne seat, now lowered so that it is at right angles to the picture plane and recedes swiftly behind the finial, heightening the sense of forms overlapping each other in space. All these features place the Florence panel at a late date.

The haloes contain a rosette stamp which occurs elsewhere in the shop of Guido, as in the *Madonna del Voto*, and the *Madonnas* in San Gimignano and Montaione. It occurs earlier in the Shutters No. 5 and the Polyptych No. 6; the elaborately stamped halo of the Fogg *St. Dominic* is a result of a later reworking. Stamping a decorative pattern on haloes is a technique which comes into extensive use only towards the end of the thirteenth century; see the discussions in Stout, Bib. 173, and in Weigelt, Bib. 194, p. 63 n. 4. Stamped ornament does not appear in any of the works attributed to Guido himself.

The painter of the Florence *Madonna* must be accounted a highly competent assistant in the shop. This work, while it has no particular sparkle, scrupulously follows the Guidesque idiom. Stylistically, it reminds us of the Polyptych No. 6 (Figs. 33, 41) and the *Madonna del Voto* (Fig. 37); unquestionably they are all by the hand of the Madonna del Voto Master. In the shape of the Madonna heads, the drawing of the features, the slight paralysis of the left cheeks, and in the shape of the hands, this similarity may be noted. The above analysis of features in the Florence *Madonna* indicates a date in the 1280's, sometime after the San Domenico Altarpiece.

BIBLIOGRAPHY

1890 Thode, Bib. 179, pp. 3, 4, 5.
1907 Cruttwell, Bib. 47, p. 5.
1911 Weigelt, Bib. 191, pp. 214, 227.
1920 Marle, Bib. 110, p. 267.
1922 Weigelt, Bib. 192, p. 281.
1923 Mather, Bib. 113, p. 61.
1923 Marle, Bib. 107, I, pp. 285-86.
1925 Florence, Bib. 66, p. 6.
1928 Florence, Bib. 67, p. 6.
1928 Weigelt, Bib. 195, pp. 203-8.
1929 Stout, Bib. 173, p. 149.

1932 Berenson, Bib. 15, p. 268.
1932 Edgell, Bib. 61, p. 33.
1932 Florence, Bib. 68, p. 23.
1934 Sandberg-Vavalà, Bib. 151, p. 268.
1936 Florence, Bib. 69, p. 20.
1950 Offner, Bib. 133, pp. 62, 72.
1951 Florence, Bib. 70, p. 21.
1953 Sandberg-Vavalà, Bib. 153, pp. 27, 29, 30, 33.
1955 Carli, Bib. 27, pp. 22, 24.

XII. *Princeton Madonna*

FIGURE 42 — Princeton University Museum No. 40 — H 76 x W 63.5 cm.

The condition is generally good, although there is some repaint in the face of the Madonna. The gold ground is somewhat rubbed.

The panel entered the collection of Princeton University in 1962. Since 1924 it had been on loan to the Museum from the collection of Dan Fellows Platt, Englewood, New Jersey. The panel was previously in the possession of P. Merloti, Siena, and before that it was in the collection of Bishop Foti, Colle di Val d'Elsa (note of F. M. Perkins in Frick Art Reference Library).

This is the only rectangular Madonna panel from Guido's shop, all the others terminating in a gable. It is also a half-length Madonna and thus joins a very large category of Dugento paintings which endures throughout the century: the rectangular, half-length Madonna (Garrison, Nos. 62-149).

The Madonna is, furthermore, of the *glykophilousa,* or affectionate, type: the Child presses his cheek against that of his mother and encircles her neck with his arm. Although this is the only example in the oeuvre of Guido, it is not uncommon in Dugento Tuscan painting. A half-length *Madonna* of the *glykophilousa* type in a rectangular panel is attributed to the Pisan School (Garrison No. 89). The ex-Figdor

Madonna (Garrison No. 62) of the Lucchese School has the same characteristics, as do the representations in the Diptych in the Uffizi (*Giottesca*, fig. 7a) attributed to the Oblate Master of the Lucchese School, and the Lucchese *Madonna* in the Tabernacle in the Stoclet collection (Fig. 109).

The painting to which the Princeton panel compares most closely, except for the *glykophilousa* element, is the half-length *Madonna* of the early thirteenth century in the Straus collection, New York (Fig. 104), attributed to Berlinghiero of Lucca. In both there is the same dark mantle covering the head and shoulders, with a golden hem below the shoulder and tassels hanging therefrom, the star on the cloth over the Madonna's brow, the Child's light, striated tunic which covers his legs. One wonders whether the Princeton panel was not painted with a Berlinghieresque prototype in mind, perhaps a half-length *Glykophilousa* by Berlinghiero's son, Bonaventura, who, as we have seen, probably influenced Guido.

The Princeton *Madonna* is the only half-length Madonna panel in the Guidesque oeuvre. Other half-length Sienese Madonnas sometimes associated with Guido bear insufficient stylistic relation to be connected with the shop of Guido. Thus a half-length *Madonna* of the end of the century in the Opera del Duomo, Siena (Garrison No. 122) borrows the rather unusual position of the Princeton Madonna's hand in support of the Child and the costume of the Madonna; otherwise, the painting may be described as a non-Guidesque, Sienese work. The *Madonna* in San Gimignano (Garrison No. 316) recalls the Guidesque system in the facial features of the Madonna but the character of the painting has little to do with Guidesque style. The *Madonna*, No. 17 in the Siena Pinacoteca (Garrison No. 121), has no relation to the Guidesque style and has, instead, been related to the St. John Altarpiece in the Siena Pinacoteca (Bib. 153, p. 56). The Sienese *Madonna* in San Francesco, Montalcino (Garrison No. 314) has only vague analogies to Guido, not enough to classify it as a work of the shop or following. Finally, the *Madonna* in the London National Gallery, part of a diptych (Garrison No. 273 and p. 107), would seem to be not Sienese but Pisan and close to the oeuvre of the SS. Cosma e Damiano Master (Garrison, p. 29).

Despite the high quality of the Princeton *Madonna* and notwithstanding a certain vivacity in the faces, it lacks, in the final analysis, the personal touch of the master. A comparison of the face of the Madonna (Fig. 93) with that in the Polyptych No. 7 (Fig. 94) is instructive. Here the schematization of the eyes is simpler, lacking those sharp contrasts of dark and white lights defining the eye socket both above and below. The nose, like the face itself, is less elongated than that in the No. 7 Polyptych, and seems blunter. The very good head of the Child, so close in some ways to the angels (Fig. 65) of the spandrels in the Palazzo Pubblico *Madonna*, is set on a neck which lacks all that tension of stretched muscles seen in the Guido figures. There is none of that rhythmic play of the strands of his hair which we saw in the hair of the Child in the No. 7 Polyptych (Fig. 66). His feet and hands are poorly drawn; especially the left hand suffers in comparison with those by Guido himself. The right hand of the Madonna is only an imitation of the hand we see in the Palazzo Pubblico *Madonna* and the Polyptych No. 7; it lacks the rhythmic sweep from the root of the thumb to the tip of the index finger and the little finger is abnormally thick.

The position of the Child's head is close to that of the Child in the Palazzo Pubblico panel; it is possible that the assistant who painted this work drew upon that work for the heads. The wealth of lush leaf and flower forms in the haloes and also the stippling of the ground between these forms are considered Ducciesque by Weigelt (Bib. 192), but actually they are almost identical to those which Guido had developed by the time he did the Palazzo Pubblico *Madonna*. This, in any event, prohibits a date before the 1280's for the Princeton *Madonna*.

The similarities of this panel to that attributed to Berlinghiero have been noted. It is curious that the other painting with which the Guidesque panel can be most closely related is from the other end of the century, the small *Madonna* by Duccio in the Stoclet collection (Marle, II, fig. 4). The affinity is less a matter of posture and motif than it is one of mood and of harmonious adjustment between the dark silhouette and the luxuriously expansive gold ground.

Certain stylistic features suggest that the painter of the Princeton panel may be the one who, at an earlier date, executed the San Bernardino *Madonna* (Figs. 92, 93). There is a proximity in the shaping of the Madonna's features as may be seen in the great, circling right eyebrow, the upper line of the eye carried far out to the left, and the schematizations under the eyes. The shape of the noses and mouths is nearly identical. In both paintings there is that sense for plastic values which is to be differentiated from Guido's more linearistic concepts. In a general way both Madonnas gaze out with a rather direct and cheerful glance. The sharpest difference between the two is the right hand of the Madonna which now has the familiar, tapering claw fingers peculiar to Guido. This may be a matter of the passage of time; in ten or so years, as the interval must be, the San Bernardino Master may have absorbed more of the master's style.

BIBLIOGRAPHY

1914   Perkins, Bib. 138, p. 97.

1916   Sirén, Bib. 168, p. 8.

1917   Sirén, Bib. 170, p. 110.

1922   Weigelt, Bib. 192, p. 282.

1923   Marle, Bib. 107, I, p. 373.

1932   Berenson, Bib. 15, p. 268.

1932   Edgell, Bib. 61, p. 33.

1933   Venturi, L., Bib. 189, pl. XII.

1949   Garrison, Bib. 73, No. 112.

1950   Offner, Bib. 133, p. 62.

1954   Shorr, Bib. 155, p. 40.

XIII. *Galli-Dunn Madonna*

FIGURE 43   Siena Pinacoteca No. 587   H 125 x W 73 cm.

Although somewhat dark in tone, the panel is in generally good condition. The gold background has been much abraded. The frame is original.

The panel came to the Pinacoteca from the collection of Prof. Marcello Galli-Dunn in 1906.

In the literature this painting has generally been considered a replica of the Palazzo Pubblico *Madonna* by an assistant of rather mediocre talent. The importance of the Galli-Dunn *Madonna* for our understanding of the great Guido *Madonna* is considerable. For one thing the decoration of the throne is typical of the Guido ambient: large, bell-shaped leaves and dainty colonnettes. That some such decorative scheme was used on the throne of the Palazzo Pubblico painting has been proven by the recent cleaning (Fig. 71). Probably the broad left side of the throne of the Palazzo Pubblico *Madonna* (Fig. 73) bore a strong resemblance to what we see in the replica. The novelty of a throne seen only from one side was not readily absorbed by all painters as is demonstrated here: this assistant shows the left side of the throne in a diagonal recession, but he also swings the right side of the throne out into full view, failing to comprehend the spatial advantage inherent in a diagonal view.

Critics have spoken of the panel as a reduction of the Palazzo Pubblico painting. It is particularly true when we realize that the Galli-Dunn panel is based on what was only the center panel of a large, complex altarpiece. The simplification process extends itself to the number of angels in the spandrels, from three to one on either side, and the omission of such details as the triangular decorations on the arc of the throneback. It seems important, as Offner (Bib. 133) has pointed out, that the single molding of the cusped arch is not just a simplification but reflects a new style of the period in which the panel must have been painted. The single, molded, cusped arch has parallels in the St. Peter Altarpiece (Fig. 53) and the Montaione *Madonna* (Fig. 54), both fairly late Guidesque works datable in the late 1280's or the 1290's. With such criteria in mind, it would be difficult to agree with Brandi (Bib. 164) that the panel dates from around 1260.

There is no secure basis for the attribution of any other Guidesque work to the Galli-Dunn painter. Undoubtedly he was already in the shop in the 1270's because he follows the formulas of Guido so closely. Like the Madonna del Voto Master, this assistant may be described as more faithful than inspired.

BIBLIOGRAPHY

1904   Siena, Bib. 166, p. 300.   1909   Siena, Bib. 162, p. 25.
1906   Franchi, Bib. 71, pp. 116-17.   1911   Weigelt, Bib. 191, p. 213.

1916 Sirén, Bib. 168, pp. 7-9.
1920 Marle, Bib. 110, p. 267.
1922 Weigelt, Bib. 192, p. 281.
1923 Marle, Bib. 107, I, pp. 366-68.
1928 Weigelt, Bib. 195, pp. 203-8.
1932 Berenson, Bib. 15, p. 269.
1932 Edgell, Bib. 61, p. 34.
1933 Siena, Bib. 164, p. 112.

1934 Sandberg-Vavalà, Bib. 151, pp. 259, 261, 268.
1950 Offner, Bib. 133, pp. 62, 65, 66.
1953 Sandberg-Vavalà, Bib. 153, pp. 23, 24, 33, 34.
1955 Carli, Bib. 28, p. 24.
1957 Stubblebine, Bib. 176, pp. 33-34.
1958 Siena, Bib. 165, p. 19.

XIV. *Courtauld Coronation of the Virgin*

FIGURES 44-47   London, the Courtauld Institute of Art No. 24   H 56 (restored) x W 164 cm.

The coats of arms seemingly held by the angels are modern. The piece of gable above the Virgin's halo is a modern replacement, following the presumed original lines. Otherwise, the panel is in fairly good condition.

In the Lord's open book may be read the following which comes from the Office of the Assumption:

VENI ELECTA MEA ET PONAM IN TE THRONUM MEUM

The panel was left to the Courtauld Institute upon the death of Viscount Lee of Fareham in 1948. It had been purchased in Italy in 1923.

In terms of what we know about thirteenth century painting, it is certain that this triangular panel is a fragment from a larger work, serving as a gable or pediment above another representation. A number of factors also indicate that the Coronation is a complete section in itself. For example, the molding around the central group is what we might call a known shape; in proportion it recalls the aedicula of the *Coronation* on the north façade of Chartres. The cusped arch was, of course, also familiar from such a work as the Palazzo Pubblico *Madonna*. Besides this, the area of the Coronation is self-sustaining, the footstools and the feet of the enthroned figures offering a logical terminus to the scene. The angels on either side, while seeming to be fragments, are compositionally complete; their wings fit the corners as neatly as do those of the spandrel and pediment angels of the Palazzo Pubblico *Madonna*. Unusual as such a segmented mandorla may be, it probably did not extend down into the lower area of the painting; nowhere is there an instance of a single mandorla framing several separate episodes. Thus, the pediment may be read as a complete composition. It may have been separated from the lower area by a painted decorative band or by a thin molding such as the one which frames the *Coronation*.

Several difficult problems are posed when we seek the shape and the iconographic program of the complete painting. Coor, who published the picture (Bib. 40), believes it is a fragment of a work, the entirety of which can be established by completing the ellipse of the mandorla which is seen in the two small segments. She believes the lower part contained an Assumption. In examining evidence for such a corollary scene, Coor believes Guido may have followed the example of the fresco by Cimabue in the upper church at Assisi in which a mandorla contains the figures of the Lord and the Virgin sitting together on an arc. However, it is difficult to imagine Guido representing the Lord and the Virgin on a throne in the *Coronation* above and repeating the same two figures seated this time on an arc in an Assumption below. As an alternate source for the lost lower part of the Guidesque panel, Coor cites the *Assumption* with the Virgin sitting alone on the arc in the Ducciesque window in the apse of the Siena Cathedral, which recent criticism (Bib. 23) has placed around 1287-88, but which is stylistically of the period of the *Maestà* or later and is thus at quite a remove from the Guidesque example.

However, in the few Italian representations of the Assumption preserved from the thirteenth century, with the exception of Cimabue's, the Virgin is represented standing. This is true of the scene in the panel by Margaritone in Monte San Savino (Garrison No. 358) in which the Virgin's mandorla is flanked by the Apostles and supported by small angels. The composition is the same in the scene in an Umbrian panel in Antwerp (Garrison No. 360) except for the omission of the mandorla. The Virgin is also represented standing in the fresco in the Church of SS. Giovanni e Paolo, Spoleto (Marle, I, fig. 320), a scene in which the ascending Virgin is shown handing her girdle to St. Thomas. These few examples, which complete the list of thirteenth century Italian *Assumptions*, suggest that Guido would also have represented the Virgin as standing. However, it should be noted that none of these *Assumptions* is accompanied by a representation of the Coronation.

More to the taste of the thirteenth century in Italy, and frequently found in northern European art, is the combination of the Dormition and the Coronation. And this is exactly what we find in the best-known example of the period, the mosaic by Jacopo Torriti in the apse of Santa Maria Maggiore, Rome, signed and dated 1295 (Fig. 106). There the Coronation is enacted in a great, round mandorla and the Dormition is represented as a long, low scene running beneath. Most remarkable in the mosaic of the Dormition is the strongly centralized position of the Lord, who stands in a half-mandorla the terminal points of which are at the head and feet of the recumbent Virgin. The hieratic Lord, holding the soul of the now-deceased Virgin, inhabits a celestial realm marked off by the mandorla, all of which is strongly reminiscent of the old Byzantine formula. It is as though this part of the composition of the Dormition were to be thought of as a separate episode, and indeed, in an early fourteenth century panel in Forlì (Garrison No. 318) by a painter who shows a penchant for Guidesque motifs, the "Master of Forlì," the mandorla containing the standing figure of the Lord carrying the soul of the Virgin is abstracted completely from the scene around the bier below and made into a separate episode above it. Certain conclusions can be drawn about the Dormition scene. In representations in which the Lord holds the soul of the Virgin, the Assumption is not depicted, except in scattered examples. Contrariwise, in sequences of the Dormition, the Assumption, and the Coronation together, the Lord does not hold the soul of the Virgin except, again, in isolated instances. Apparently the representation of the Lord holding the soul of the Virgin stood in lieu of an Assumption. This is, of course, a corruption of the tradition in which, after the soul is borne to Heaven, it is returned to the body and the Virgin is then assumed, body and soul, into Heaven. As represented in art the program is complete if the Dormition contains an intimation of resurrection, namely the Lord holding the soul of the Virgin. The probability is, then, that the Guidesque *Coronation* originally would have surmounted not an Assumption but a Dormition, in which the Lord holding the soul of the Virgin would have been given a certain emphasis.

It is likely that an Italian prototype existed for both the Guidesque panel and the Torriti mosaic (Fig. 106). It is interesting to see that Coor was struck by the similarities between the panel and the mosaic in such matters as the color scheme, the figures, the crown, and the inscription in the book, which, as Coor points out, contains identical words from the Office of the Assumption. She suggests that Torriti may have known the Guidesque work. It may be well though to seek, through the qualities they share, a common ancestry. The postures of the figures in the Guidesque work, especially that of the Virgin, recall the robust contrapposto of the figure in the Orvieto *Madonna* (Fig. 81) of the late 1260's by Coppo di Marcovaldo. Something of that vigor may be noted as well in the figure of the Lord in Torriti's version. In the mosaic there are even more interesting, because more obscure, reminiscences of Coppo's Orvieto *Madonna*: the lyre-back throne and the double cushion on which the figures sit. In both representations we find a frontal throne despite the fact that they were both executed in the era of the diagonal throne. Both the Guidesque and the Torriti throne would seem to reflect the style of throne in Coppo di Marcovaldo, still frontal and with limited suggestions of three-dimensionality. The curious slits in both thrones, seen also in the *Coronation of the Virgin* at Chartres and the Santa Maria in Trastevere mosaic (Bib. 182, fig. 622), may also be supposed for this lost prototype. It is conceivable that Coppo may have painted a large-scale panel of the Coronation and Dormition in Umbria, possibly in Assisi where both Torriti and Guido seem to have been.

The restoration of the original shape of the Guidesque panel also poses problems. Coor suggested a panel shape similar to the shape of the Ascension mosaic on the façade of San Frediano, Lucca (Fig. 107). The proportions of the Courtauld gable are lower and broader than those of Guido's gable in the Palazzo Pubblico (Fig. 15) from which we may gather that the over-all shape of the picture was a fairly low and broad gabled dossal. This would have been well suited to the horizontal composition of the usual Dormition, just as it would have been ill-suited to the vertical orientation of the typical Assumption. Something of the scale of the figures in the lost scene can be gauged from the pediment angels; clearly they must have been of a scale equal to if not larger than that of the angels. The lost scene, which constituted the principal episode of the panel, would have been a larger composition while the Coronation would have served as a more diminutive gable theme, just the reverse of Torriti's emphasis in his 1295 mosaic.

After all this has been said, it must be added, finally, that we cannot entirely rule out the possibility that the pediment crowned a Madonna and Child or some other devotional image. No earlier examples of such a combination can be adduced since this is the earliest preserved Coronation in Italian painting. However, we do have the combination in an important work which followed, Duccio's *Maestà* of 1308-11. There, as we believe, the central pinnacle, directly above the Madonna and Child, depicted the Dormition of the Virgin and was capped by a triangular piece showing the Coronation of the Virgin, in all probability without the intervening episode of the Assumption. Were the Guidesque *Coronation* the pediment of an altarpiece, the over-all effect would probably have been similar to that of the San Domenico Altarpiece.

The panel probably should be dated in the 1280's. Other works with such thin interior moldings occur no earlier than that decade. The throne, too, despite its archaic frontality and tipped-up seat, betrays its lateness in the forward terminal posts which boldly overlap the seat of the throne.

The panel is the work of a capable assistant, otherwise unknown, who gives every indication of being an old hand with Guidesque formulas and who, in this instance, may have been working on a design by Guido himself. The striations on the robes of the enthroned figures are very much as Guido would have manipulated them. But in the faces of the angels there is a certain heavyhandedness we could not attribute to the master. It is as though the painter strove for something of that vigor we find in Coppo's angels. The face of the Virgin, satisfactorily modeled, lacks nevertheless that flicker of animation to which we are accustomed in Guido's personal oeuvre.

BIBLIOGRAPHY

1957   Coor, Bib. 40, pp. 328-30.   1960   London, Bib. 98, p. 6.
1959   London, Bib. 99, p. 12.   1961   Oertel, Bib. 128, p. 67.

XV. *Fogg St. Dominic*

FIGURE 48   Cambridge, Massachusetts, Fogg Art Museum No. 1920.20   H 115 x W 61.5 cm.

The panel originally represented a full-length figure, the lower part having been cut off at an undetermined time. Recent X rays reveal the presence of two other, earlier faces underneath the one presently visible; in addition, there has been discovered another pair of hands which conform in contour with the present ones. These observations were made by Millard Meiss, Elizabeth H. Jones, Chief Conservator at the Fogg Museum, and Carmen Gómez-Moreno, who plan to publish the results of the laboratory tests in the near future. During the recent restoration the back of the panel was infused with wax and covered with a strong layer of linen. The surface is much rubbed and there are scattered damages. The halo is apparently later in date.

The panel came to the Fogg in 1920 from the collection of F. M. Perkins at Lastra a Signa. The provenance is very likely a church of the Dominican Order.

This representation is considered by Kaftal (Bib. 91) to be the earliest extant image of St. Dominic; however, it is probably antedated by the image of him in the Gallerani Shutters (Fig. 35) of ca. 1275, and as well by the representations in the Florentine Tabernacle at Yale (Marle, I, fig. 192) and that in a *Madonna* by the Magdalen Master (Garrison No. 177), both of which probably date in the early 1270's. There are two panels of the full-length St. Dominic in Naples (Garrison Nos. 169 and 337), both from the Campanian school and both from the latter part of the century.

A full-length saint in a gabled panel is relatively rare in the painting of the period. The earlier mode for representing a single figure of a saint is seen in the numerous rectangular panels of Margaritone d'Arezzo (Garrison, pp. 50-52). Although gabled dossals appear at a much earlier date, for example the 1235 *St. Francis* (Fig. 62) by Bonaventura Berlinghieri in Pescia, there is no certain evidence of the use of the gabled panel for a Madonna or single figure representation before the 1270's.

The shape of the Fogg panel is of great importance for determining its date of origin. While we assume the lower part of the panel was cut off because there are no three-quarter length figures in the thirteenth century, there is no indication that lateral areas were cut off. Otherwise, we could presume there may have been lateral scenes from the life of St. Dominic, thus relating this painting in its original shape to the Pescia *St. Francis* and allowing a date anywhere in the thirteenth century. As it is, we must assume the original shape was a vertical, gabled panel containing only a single, full-length Saint. Although we can find panels of single saints without scenes from their legends in the early part of the century such as the *St. Francis* in the Louvre (Bib. 135, fig. 3) and the venerated *St. Francis* by the St. Francis Master (Fig. 105), as well as the works of that retardataire master, Margaritone d'Arezzo, they are all cast in a rectangular format. It is noteworthy that only towards the end of the thirteenth century is a gabled shape used for the representation of a single, standing saint, and the only example, other than the Guidesque work, is the *St. Luke* by the Magdalen Master (*Giottesca*, fig. 71a), which dates no earlier than the 1280's.

The Dominican prohibition against decoration of all sorts during the earlier part of the thirteenth century (Bib. 106) strengthens the belief that such an image as the Fogg *St. Dominic* was not created before the 1280's. The absence of earlier paintings of St. Dominic either as a single figure or as the center of an historiated dossal is in striking contrast to the great number of such representations of St. Francis produced throughout the thirteenth century.

The pose of the Saint would seem to offer little clue to the dating of the panel. While the hieratic posture of the right hand is close to that of the 1235 *St. Francis* in Pescia, it is a constant during the thirteenth century, often found in the works of the Magdalen Master and, as well, in early fourteenth century Sienese painting, notably a Ducciesque representation of St. Dominic in Chicago (Bib. 20, fig. 119).

Perhaps the surest guide to the late date of the *St. Dominic* is the luxurious space in which the figure is placed. By contrast the Louvre *St. Francis* of the 1230's is constricted within a much smaller space as can be seen at the top where the halo and head-cape lap up over the framing. Even Coppo, in his Siena *Madonna* of 1261, did not constrain his halo entirely to the picture surface, although he was more successful at this in the Orvieto *Madonna* later in the same decade. In the Guidesque work, it is the gable shape which creates a generous space around the figure of the Saint; this factor places the Fogg picture close to the Palazzo Pubblico *Madonna* where the same spatial idea is so important.

Unfortunately the X rays reveal too little of the two earlier images for us to make clear stylistic analyses. The earlier faces do not coincide with each other or with the present face, so that the repaintings also involved major relocations of the image. The earlier hands, however, follow the same lines as the present ones.

Ordinarily, it would seem logical to assume that the repaintings of the panel were spaced at intervals of some years and were due either to the result of damage and wear of the surface or the desire for an up-to-date image. Nothing about the latest of the three faces, however, leads us to suppose a date later than ca. 1290. The painter adheres closely to the Guidesque formulas seen in such typically Guidesque works as the Shutters No. 5 (Figs. 35, 36) or the Grosseto *Last Judgment* (Fig. 49). Thus we are forced to presume two repaintings of the image within a period of not much more than a decade.

The problem of the panel is further compounded by the nature of the halo decoration. Stout has observed that the tooling of this halo follows practices of the early fourteenth century (Bib. 173); instead of the engraving technique customary in the thirteenth century we find the use of six different stamps. It is noteworthy that the small, pointed pattern around the perimeter of the halo does not appear even in Duccio but is everywhere in the ambient of Simone Martini. Since the tooling is so much later than the painting style, Stout very rightly wonders whether the background may not have been regilded and retooled during the first quarter of the fourteenth century.

The new face of St. Dominic, in other words, is not of the same period as the new halo; they are the results of different refurbishings. If the face of St. Dominic which we see today on this panel had been painted in the early fourteenth century, we would expect it to bear a much closer resemblance to that of the St. Francis in the dossal from Guido's shop (Fig. 61), a work of the early fourteenth century.

Perhaps a clue to this elaborate puzzle would be provided if we knew more of the history of the picture. If, for example, it was an important devotional image in a Dominican church, possibly even on an altar in San Domenico, Siena, this might account for all the attention it received. It would not be an isolated instance.

The painter responsible for the latest of the images in this palimpsest is an assistant who follows rather faithfully the Guido formula for the bearded, male ascetic. He cannot, however, be identified with any specific hand in the shop.

BIBLIOGRAPHY

1923 Marle, Bib. 107, I, p. 377.
1927 Harvard, Bib. 82, p. 44.
1929 Stout, Bib. 173, pp. 141-52.
1932 Berenson, Bib. 15, p. 268.

1932 Edgell, Bib. 61, pp. 32, 33, 35.
1936 Harvard, Bib. 83, p. 69.
1948 Kaftal, Bib. 91, p. 20.
1952 Kaftal, Bib. 90, pp. 309-12.

XVI. *Grosseto Last Judgment*

FIGURES 49, 113   Grosseto, Museo Diocesano d'Arte Sacra   H 140 x W 99 cm.

The panel has been cut at the bottom, but with small loss. There is a vertical split on the right side. The panel was restored in 1954 at which time flaking surfaces were consolidated.

The inscription on either side of the cross reads:

SURGITE MORTUI   VENITE AD IUDICIU[M]

The inscription is erroneously given as "SURGITE AD AUDIENDUM IUDICIUM" in the 1904 exhibition catalogue and in Weigelt (Bib. 191).

The panel was transferred to the Museo Diocesano d'Arte Sacra in 1932-33 from the Oratorio della Misericordia, Grosseto. In 1904 and 1907 it was mentioned as being in the Cathedral of Grosseto.

The depiction of the Last Judgment in Dugento Tuscan painting is rare although van Marle (Bib. 112) errs in believing the Grosseto example unique in panel painting. The upper part of the picture is dominated by a majestic Christ sitting on a rainbow throne in a mandorla, surrounded by trumpeting angels. Beneath the feet of Christ we see the prominent cross; this is the earliest known example of the motif in a representation of the Last Judgment in Italian painting (Bib. 132), although a sculptured example was near at hand in the Pisani Pulpit in the Siena Cathedral. On the right, below, the Damned rise from their graves only to plunge into Hell. To the left below the Saved also rise and are led to Paradise by St. Peter. This, too, is the first instance of the episode in Italian painting (Bib. 132).

It is as though the Christ were created in some plastic medium, so forcibly does the figure stand forth from the surrounding area. By contrast the angels appear paper-thin. The effect reminds us of the Christ in relief in the 1215 Altarpiece in the Siena Pinacoteca. The intention must have been to enhance the iconic value by sculpturesque treatment.

An important representation of the Last Judgment is that of the Florence Baptistery (Fig. 108). There Christ wears a tunic under his mantle so that his right arm and shoulder are covered. His left hand turns down in a gesture of rejection. These features are also found in the Tabernacle in the Metropolitan Museum, New York, by the Magdalen Master (Marle, I, fig. 191) and later, in the Arena Chapel fresco by Giotto (Marle, III, fig. 66). The tunic and the gesture of the left hand become Florentine characteristics, at least in contrast to the formula in Guido's shop where the mantle of Christ leaves bare the right side of his torso and his entire right arm. In the Guidesque work, two jets of blood curve out from the wound in Christ's side. Both arms are extended and both palms turned out, revealing the wounds.

Ultimately certain features of the Grosseto *Last Judgment* are traceable to the representations in tympana of French Gothic Cathedrals of the twelfth and thirteenth centuries, such as St. Denis, Laon, Paris, Amiens, Rheims and Bourges. In all these examples, Christ's right side is invariably bare and his arms are outstretched with palms out to reveal the wounds. Except that his left arm is lower, the Last Judgment Christ on the Pulpit in the Siena Cathedral also follows this formula. Examples of this northern type appear in two paintings of the Lucchese school. The earlier one is a scene in a Tabernacle in the Stoclet Collection (Fig. 109) of the second quarter of the thirteenth century, which is stylistically close to Berlinghiero. The other example occurs on a pair of shutters (*Giottesca*, pp. 34-35) in Berlin attributed to Deodato Orlandi or his following. It seems that the French formula was taken up by the Pisani and the Lucchese school but not by the Florentine school. Once again, we are struck by the correspondence between Guido and the Pisani and the school of Lucca and not, significantly, with the Florentine school.

A number of stylistic similarities relate this work to the oeuvre of the St. Peter Master, which includes the Reliquary Shutters No. 5 (Figs. 35, 36) and the St. Peter Altarpiece (Fig. 53). Most revealing is the treatment of architectural elements. In the episode of the Blessed Led to Paradise the flatness of the arch beneath the stairs and of the baldacchino above the figures is comparable to what we see in the other two works. The steps turn into the picture plane, thus losing all sense of substantiality; this is analogous to the three flat steps under the feet of the central figure in the St. Peter Altarpiece.

The treatment of drapery is also very close to that in his other works. The tunic of Christ has folds described by long brushstrokes in a darker tone. The angels (Fig. 113) are swathed in white with gathered folds of a type found in comparable figures in the St. Peter Altarpiece (Figs. 111, 115).

Schematizations of the face of Christ likewise recall those in the other works of the St. Peter Master. The sparseness of Christ's beard and the dark ringlets against the neck are found in the image of Beato Andrea in the *Gallerani Distributing Alms* (Fig. 114) and, in the other work, in the *Calling of Peter* (Fig. 53). The faces of the angels in the *Last Judgment* are more schematized than those in the St. Peter Altarpiece, suggesting an earlier date for the Grosseto panel. On the other hand, their light fabrics and graceful, almost Gothic poses would seem to be later than the effects created in the Gallerani Shutters. We have proposed a date of ca. 1275 for the Shutters and a date at the end of the 1280's for the St. Peter Altarpiece. The Grosseto panel should be placed somewhere between these two works and may be dated approximately 1280. For a fuller discussion of the evolution of this master's style, see Cat. No. XIX below.

BIBLIOGRAPHY

1904 Siena, Bib. 166, p. 300.
1907 Venturi, Bib. 188, v, pp. 113-14.
1910 Nicolosi, Bib. 127, p. 117.
1911 Weigelt, Bib. 191, p. 226.
1920 Marle, Bib. 110, p. 269.
1921 Marle, Bib. 112, p. 253.
1923 Marle, Bib. 107, I, p. 373.
1923 Touring Club Italiano, Bib. 183, III, p. 160.
1927 Toesca, Bib. 182, p. 994.
1932 Berenson, Bib. 15, p. 268.
1935 Touring Club Italiano, Bib. 184, p. 600.

1941 Coletti, Bib. 35, p. lxii n. 49.
1943 *Giottesca*, Bib. 167, pp. 96-97.
1944 Coor, Bib. 41, p. 148.
1946 Carli, Bib. 26, p. 26.
1947 Offner, Bib. 132, Sect. III, vol. v, p. 252 n. 6, p. 257 nn. 16, 18.
1948 Longhi, Bib. 100, p. 36.
1949 Garrison, Bib. 73, No. 159.
1951 Meiss, Bib. 117, p. 76 n. 13.
1955 Carli, Bib. 27, pp. 39-40.
1955 Carli, Bib. 28, p. 30.
1961 DeWald, Bib. 59, p. 79.

XVII. *Memphis Polyptych: Madonna and Child with Four Saints: Mary Magdalen, Savino, Unidentified Apostle, Margaret of Antioch*

FIGURES 50, 51, 122   Memphis, Tennessee, Brooks Memorial Art Gallery,   H 100 x W 190 cm.
Samuel H. Kress Collection

The frame and moldings are modern although they probably reflect the original design, except for the curious modern corbels affixed to the cusps. The panel was restored by the Kress Foundation in the 1950's at which time horizontal breaks on a level with the Virgin's mouth and her right fingers were repaired, as well as the abraded area along the bottom of the panel. There are scattered damages and repainting.

The panel was purchased for the Kress Foundation in 1952 and presented to the Brooks Memorial Art Gallery in 1958. Before coming to America the panel was in the collection of Lodovico Rosselli, Rome; previously, it can successively be traced back to the collection of Principe del Drago, Rome, the Stettiner Collection, Rome, the Odescalchi Collection (?), Rome, and, finally, the Piccolomini Collection, Siena. The Sienese provenance is confirmed by the presence of San Savino, one of the city's patron saints (see Bib. 90, cols. 29-32).

The Guidesque character of this Polyptych is established at once by the presence of the cusped arch over the Madonna. The motif of the angels spread-winged in the spandrels already appeared in the Polyptych No. 6. Unlike Polyptychs No. 6 and No. 7, this was designed in just five compartments. The arches extend farther down than in the other examples, thus tending to isolate each figure in its compartment. This is so similar to the stage of development in Vigoroso's Polyptych of 128 . . . (Fig. 75) and in the Madonna del Voto Polyptych (Fig. 38) that they must be considered close in date. The disparity in size between the Madonna and the saints strikes a certain provincial note, as, indeed, does the infelicitous posture of the Christ Child and the drawing of his limbs.

Garrison (Bib. 74) attributes the painting to his "Montaione Master" but the formal concepts of the painter of the Polyptych are totally divergent. Rather than having an affinity with the Montaione *Madonna*, which we attribute to the St. Peter Master (Cat. No. XX), this Polyptych should be included in the oeuvre of the painter who executed the *Lord and Virgin Enthroned* (Fig. 34), the so-called Clarisse Master. Also attributable to the Clarisse Master are the Krakow Tabernacle (Figs. 56-58) and the San Gimignano Cross (Fig. 55). The identity of formal characteristics in the *Lord and Virgin Enthroned* (Fig. 123) and the Memphis Polyptych (Fig. 122) can be seen in such things as the formation of the hands: doughy, over-musculated fingers and bulge of muscle at the root of the thumb, features already observed in the Madonna of the Polyptych and the Christ of the Clarisse painting. The hard, carven features are the same in both, while the loop of the ear of the Madonna in the Polyptych is identical to that of the Virgin in the Clarisse panel. Again, the very narrow oval of the iris which floats against the white of the eye is the same. It is not difficult to find these characteristics in the San Gimignano Cross (Fig. 121). In the case of the Krakow Tabernacle (Fig. 57), its bad condition cannot hide that certain awkwardness and stiffness in his rendering of bodily forms.

This assistant is closest to Guido in the earlier Clarisse panel. In the Polyptych he has begun to diverge from the shop, a process that will be even more noticeable in the San Gimignano Crucifix and the Krakow Tabernacle. One would surmise that his relationship to the shop was rather tangential at the point in his career when he painted this Polyptych, very likely in the 1280's.

BIBLIOGRAPHY

1938 Venturi, A. (in Marle, Bib. 109, pp. 347-58).

1947 Garrison, Bib. 74, pp. 300-3.
1949 Garrison, Bib. 73, p. 23 and No. 434.

1950   Offner, Bib. 133, p. 65.   1961   Emerson, Bib. 62, pp. 837, 843.
1958   Memphis, Bib. 119, pp. 8-9.

XVIII. *Yale Crucifixion*

FIGURE 52   New Haven, Connecticut, Yale University Gallery,   H 58 x W 96.5 cm.
                                Jarves Collection No. 2

The lateral edges of the panel are rough. The point of the panel at the top has
been lost. There is a horizontal break at the level of Christ's waist. The stones from
his halo are lacking. Although the picture has some damages and losses of surface
color, as in the green of the ground level, it is in good condition after the cleaning
of several years ago.

J. J. Jarves brought this and other pictures to America in 1860 and sold the collection to Yale University in 1871. He found the painting in a church near Siena;
he claimed it was painted for the position over the doorway where he found it.

Jarves' supposition (Bib. 89) that it was painted for a doorway is unlikely. The
shape as we see it is not possible in the thirteenth century. Sirén (Bib. 169) was the
first to suggest that the panel might have been a gable crowning an altarpiece.
Although there is no close analogy for the use of a Crucifixion scene in a pediment,
scattered examples are found for some time to come (Marle, v, figs. 24, 55 and 279;
see also Bib. 132, Section III, vol. v, p. 52 n. 1). If the panel were originally made as
a triangular pediment, the sides were cut off later.

The greater likelihood, however, is that the fragment we are looking at is complete
in width. The building at the left and the man crouching at the right are compositional brackets and clearly intended as such. We have, then, a fragment of a gabled
panel of the present width which extended down to contain another representation.
We should visualize the Crucifixion scene as extending downward beyond the area
of the gable proper and encroaching on the main part of a rectangular panel below.
The change of direction from the slope of the gable to the vertical of the sides is
recognized in the composition; the top of the parapet wall articulates this transition
from a triangular to a rectangular area. The lower portion might have contained
either a Madonna Enthroned, a usual complement to the Crucifixion in diptychs,
or else small narratives: the Flagellation or the Mounting of the Cross and the Deposition.

There are strong compositional affinities to the *Crucifixion* (Fig. 28) from the
Badia Ardenga group. By a process of simplification and reduction, the milling crowd
to the right of the cross has been reduced to four figures. The Christ figure is close
to that in the Badia Ardenga scene in proportions, in schematizations of the face
and torso, and in the *perizoma*. On the other hand, the position of the legs of Christ,

with the right crossed over the left, and the feet held by one nail, is more like what we find in the figure of Christ in the San Gimignano Cross (Fig. 55), a late work of the shop where non-Guidesque influences are at work. This motif might come, however, from the Siena Cathedral Pulpit of the 1260's by the Pisani; Weigelt (Bib. 192) has already pointed out the fact that the crouching figure to the right seems to be derived from that source. If so, it would be one of several references by Guido or his shop to this important monument.

The derivation of certain elements in this scene from the Badia Ardenga *Crucifixion* prevents a date earlier than the 1280's for this panel; in fact, a date at the end of that decade would be most logical. Most critics assign the panel to the shop although Sirén (Bib. 169) gives it to the master himself. While the faces of the Marys, the kneeling Magdalen, and the St. John reveal basic Guidesque traits, they are distinguishable from those by Guido and his closer followers by a somber aspect, static expressions, and a dry quality in the painting. No other major panel can be ascribed to this painter; possibly he is one of those who contributed to the Badia Ardenga scenes in certain parts left to the assistants. For example, the St. John of this painting recalls the same figure in the Badia Ardenga *Deposition* (Fig. 29); the patterning of the hair and the shape of the features are very close. Guido, on the other hand, would have made more felicitous groupings, avoiding such a diminutive group as we see at the right. Nevertheless he is a good assistant, well acquainted with the shop traditions. The relative closeness of this panel to Guido makes us realize how far from the master is such a work as the *Crucifixion* in Leningrad (Bib. 43, fig. 6) despite its derivation from a Guidesque prototype, while the *Crucifixion* in Lucignano (Garrison No. 262) seems not even to be Sienese.

BIBLIOGRAPHY

1861	Jarves, Bib. 88, p. 114.	1922	Weigelt, Bib. 192, p. 284.
1861	Jarves, Bib. 89, p. 6.	1927	Offner, Bib. 134, pp. 2, 37.
1868	Sturgis, Bib. 177, pp. 24-25.	1932	Berenson, Bib. 15, p. 268.
1905	Rankin, Bib. 141, p. 7.	1932	Edgell, Bib. 61, p. 33.
1915	Sirén, Bib. 169, pp. 277-79.	1949	Garrison, Bib. 73, No. 298.
1916	Sirén, Bib. 168, pp. 7-9.	1951	Meiss, Bib. 118, p. 150 n. 80.
1917	Sirén, Bib. 170, p. 110.	1953	Coor, Bib. 43, pp. 257-58.
1920	Marle, Bib. 110, p. 270.		

XIX. *St. Peter Altarpiece.* CENTER: *St. Peter Enthroned*; LATERAL NARRATIVES: *Annunciation, Nativity, Calling of Peter, Peter Liberated from Prison, Fall of Simon Magus, Crucifixion of Peter*

FIGURES 53, 111, 112, 115   Siena Pinacoteca No. 15   H 100 x W 141 cm.

The horizontal fracture across the panel at the level of St. Peter's shoulder is the chief damage. Much of the surface has been abraded, most seriously in the *Fall of*

Simon Magus and the *Crucifixion of Peter* where several figures have been scratched out.

The inscription on either side of the head of St. Peter reads:

· S · PE TRUS

The painting was already listed as No. 15 in the Siena Catalogue of 1864. It came to the Pinacoteca from the church of San Pietro in Banchi, now demolished, where it was seen in 1782 by Della Valle. However, in 1812 Da Morrona claims to have seen it in San Giovannino in 1792 after which, he says, it went to San Pietro in Banchi.

Such altarpieces with an enthroned saint in the central compartment are uncommon but not unknown. Comparison with the St. John Altarpiece, No. 14 in the Siena Pinacoteca, is inevitable inasmuch as both are rectangular dossals with a central enthroned saint flanked by scenes from his legend. The non-Guidesque painter of the St. John panel also shares that curious expanding perspective in the sides of his throne but is otherwise independent of the Guidesque work. Other important examples of such altarpieces with an enthroned central figure are the St. Michael panel (*Giottesca*, fig. 56a) from Vico l'Abate and the St. Zenobius Altarpiece (*Giottesca*, fig. 52a) in the Opera del Duomo, Florence, both of the Florentine School. The earliest preserved Sienese example is the Altarpiece dated 1215 in the Siena Pinacoteca, with a figure of Christ seated in a mandorla.

The figure of St. Peter is set under a cusped arch above which there is a half-length angel in either spandrel, probably to be interpreted as a borrowing from and simplification of the arrangement in the Palazzo Pubblico *Madonna*. The arch has a single thin molding, of a type found in several other Guidesque works (Figs. 37, 43, 54) which are to be dated no earlier than the 1280's.

The throne of the Saint is more developed than those which adhere to the Palazzo Pubblico Madonna formula in that its forms are lighter and thinner and one even glimpses a bit of gold ground between the legs of the throne at the left, an innovation which is probably to be attributed to Duccio, as in his *Madonna of the Three Franciscans* (Fig. 127). The rear terminals of the throne and the arch of the throneback imitate the wood-lathed parts which we see in Cimabue's *Madonna with St. Francis* (Fig. 72) in the lower church at Assisi and, later, in the 1285 Rucellai *Madonna* (Fig. 125). The painter of the St. Peter panel does not, of course, understand the idea of recession so that his throne is simply an arrangement of flat shapes. Grappling with the idea of a receding diagonal, he ends up with a throne both sides of which recede in an expanding perspective.

The space spreads easily around the figure of the seated Saint as it does around the Madonna in the Palazzo Pubblico panel and this, as much as the use of the cusped arch and superposed angels and the newfangled throne styling, suggests a date in the late 1280's. Advanced too is the three-stepped footstool which reflects contemporary concern with the problem of achieving mobility in the figure set in a contrapposto posture. In that very period the solution was being found in an adjustment of the furniture; in the multi-stepped footstools of Cimabue and Duccio one foot can be placed on an upper step thus justifying that raised leg. Without any comprehension of the three-dimensional properties of those footstools the painter of the St. Peter panel uses the device to raise the left foot and leg of the Saint but the forms remain flat shapes.

A confrontation of this central enthroned figure with the *St. Peter* in the Church of SS. Simone and Guida, Florence, attributed to the St. Cecilia Master (*Giottesca*, fig. 120), which bears the date 1307, reveals some remarkable similarities: the placing of the figure with raised left foot and leg, the head and hair, and the blessing gesture of the right hand. There may be a connection, perhaps through such a common prototype as may have been supplied by the bronze *St. Peter* in the Basilica of Saint Peter's, Rome.

For a number of critics the St. Peter Altarpiece marks the high point of Guidesque painting. Carli (Bib. 26) calls the panel the ultimate refinement of Guido's style. Brandi (Bib. 164) attributes the panel to Guido himself, considering it the most mature and perfect work of the Guidesque ambient. Sandberg-Vavalà (Bib. 153) believes it is a "better, more progressive work" than Guido's own. A number of critics (Bacci, Bib. 7 and Weigelt, Bib. 194 and Bib. 193) have characterized it as transitional between Guido and Duccio, and as very close to the early Duccio.

Certain elements of the central figure of St. Peter are derived from Guido, especially from his figure of the Redeemer in the Palazzo Pubblico gable (Fig. 15); the schematization of the bridge of the nose and brow is similar and, even more, the blessing right hand. As is usual with assistants of Guido, there is none of the master's brilliancy in the handling of draperies. A comparison between the draperies of the Saint and those of the Redeemer in the Palazzo Pubblico panel only convinces us of the extraordinary felicity of Guido's own work. In the art of painting we admire most that drapery which suggests the forms beneath while abounding in harmonious patterns of folds and striations. In the St. Peter work, the drapery is merely satisfactory in this regard, although from another viewpoint, as we shall see, it is extremely interesting.

The central figure is of monumental scale in contrast to the miniaturistic figures in the flanking narratives. Naturally, the problems with which the artist was involved differed considerably but here too an analysis of these scenes persuades us of the differences from Guido's own work and suggests the hand of an assistant working somewhat later than the period in which Guido created the Badia Ardenga scenes. A comparison with the latter is inevitable, given the thematic and compositional similarities in several of the episodes.

In the *Annunciation* (Fig. 18) from the Badia Ardenga group, schematic patterns are etched sharply on the darker tones of the drapery. Delightful as designs, these schematizations also convey a great deal of the bulk and movement of the limbs underneath as, for example, the right thigh of the Virgin and the right leg of the angel. In the *Annunciation* (Fig. 111) of the St. Peter Altarpiece, the different aspect of the drapery is due in part to the blonder tonality found throughout the work; but it is also due to a dissimilar technique and concept of form. The tunics of both the figures are conceived, not in terms of superimposed linear description, but in terms of light and dark. The diaphanous fabrics are either filled with light or gathered in shadowy folds, as between the legs of the Virgin. It may be called a painterly approach to distinguish it from Guido's linear style. But the difference may be due to more than artistic capacity or preference; probably this painter was influenced by those light, filmy, tinted fabrics of the early Duccio, such as we see on the angels in the Rucellai *Madonna* (Fig. 125). In any case, the new coloring, the thin fabrics, and the painterly approach are unlike anything we find in Guido himself and remove this Altarpiece from his personal oeuvre. On the other hand, these draperies as well as those of Peter in the scene of his liberation from prison are quite successful expressions of this new artistic personality and the forces influencing him.

Other factors distinguish this panel from Guido's own work. The architectural elements in the same Annunciation scene are noticeably flat; the artist seems to have no interest in three-dimensional forms. Even the fenestrations obtrude and somehow make the buildings seem less real. It is difficult to follow Sandberg-Vavalà's opinion (Bib. 153) that the Princeton *Annunciation* from the Badia Ardenga group is a simplification of the one in the St. Peter Altarpiece. The reverse would seem to be true. The deletion of the tree, which brought the figures of the Badia Ardenga scene together in one rhythmic sweep, is certainly part of a simplification process. The overlapping of the angel's halo and dark wing, exciting in Guido, is patently a borrowed item in the St. Peter narrative. Both figures have lost the verve which Guido gave them in his rendition; we no longer find the angel explosive or the Virgin dramatic.

The painter of the St. Peter Altarpiece can in all probability be identified with the one who painted the Gallerani Shutters (Figs. 35, 36). This was suggested by Bacci (Bib. 7) but his attribution was careless and vague. Such differences as there are between these two works may be accounted for by the passage of time; it would seem that the Gallerani scenes were painted considerably earlier than the St. Peter narratives. A substratum remains which draws the works together.

The conception of architectural forms is the same in these two works; one can compare the buildings in the exterior scene of the Shutters (Fig. 36) with those of the *Annunciation* (Fig. 111). There is the same contrast between light walls and dark fenestrations. The thin lines marking off the stories of the buildings are white on one side and black on the other as in Guido's own work but in the two works ascribed to the St. Peter Master the white and black lines curiously run in parallel channels. The decorative scroll seen in the wall of the prison of St. Peter (Fig. 115) is found again in the Shutters (Fig. 36), though nowhere else in Guidesque work.

The same weakness in drawing hands noted in the scene of Gallerani Distributing Alms (Fig. 114) recurs in the *Annunciation* (Fig. 111), the *Nativity,* and the *Calling of Peter* (Fig. 112). Certain heads of the St. Peter scenes repeat closely the types found in the Gallerani scenes. Thus, the head of Christ in the *Calling of Peter* resembles that of Gallerani in the scene of Gallerani Distributing Alms, while the spandrel angels and the angel seen twice in the *Liberation from Prison* are related, feature for feature, to the beardless young mendicants on the exterior of the Shutters.

Again, in the treatment of drapery, we find the same painterly approach. In *Gallerani Receiving Mendicants* (Fig. 36) the draperies have simple folds with shadows brushed in in a darker tone. The only significant difference in the later Altarpiece is the lighter tone, which has already been accounted for.

The community of style in these two panels points very strongly to an assistant who was close to Guido in the 1270's when he executed the No. 5 Shutters and who may have been very much more independent when he painted the St. Peter Altarpiece. That this latter work can have been executed no earlier than the end of the 1280's, and may possibly be of even later date, is made clear from its dependence on the San Domenico Altarpiece as well as the apparent Ducciesque influence. To the St. Peter Master, certainly the most original of the Guidesque, are also attributed the Gallerani Shutters (Figs. 35, 36) of ca. 1275, the Grosseto *Last Judgment* (Fig. 49), a work of the early 1280's, and the Montaione *Madonna* (Fig. 54), which dates from the end of the 1280's or even later.

Thus, as in the case of the Clarisse Master, it is possible to detect a particular personality among Guido's assistants and, once again, to observe the relaxation of ties with the shop. While the supervision of the master can easily be supposed in such a work as the Gallerani Shutters, it becomes more difficult to do so in the case of the St. Peter Altarpiece where the Guidesque formulas are very much loosened, if not substantially replaced.

BIBLIOGRAPHY

1782 Della Valle, Bib. 56, I, pp. 210-17.	1907 Jacobsen, Bib. 85, pp. 15-16.
1792 Da Morrona, Bib. 50 (in second ed., 1812, II, pp. 147-48).	1907 Venturi, Bib. 188, V, pp. 87-88.
	1911 Weigelt, Bib. 191, pp. 33, 200, 226.
1792 Lanzi, Bib. 94 (ed. 1815-16, I, p. 301).	1911 Dalton, Bib. 48, p. 322 n. 2.
1864 Siena, Bib. 158, p. 9.	1912 Lusini, Bib. 102, pp. 106-7.
1864 Crowe and Cavalcaselle, Bib. 46, I, p. 178.	1912 De Nicola, Bib. 57, pp. 10, 11.
	1915 Sirén, Bib. 169, p. 278.
1890 Thode, Bib. 179, p. 14.	1916 Sirén, Bib. 168, p. 8.
1895 Siena, Bib. 160, p. 9.	1916 Millet, Bib. 121, pp. 105, 684-85.
1903 Douglas, Bib. 60, I, p. 157 n.	1920 Marle, Bib. 111, p. 59.

1920	Marle, Bib. 110, p. 271.		1937	Meiss, Bib. 115, p. 18.
1922	Weigelt, Bib. 192, p. 282.		1937	Oertel, Bib. 130, p. 221.
1923	Marle, Bib. 107, 1, p. 382.		1937	Coletti, Bib. 34, p. 54.
1923	Mather, Bib. 113, p. 63.		1939	Bacci, Bib. 7, p. 31.
1924	Siena, Bib. 163, p. 10.		1941	Coletti, Bib. 35, 1, pp. xxvii-xxviii, xxix.
1927	Toesca, Bib. 182, p. 995.		1943	Giottesca, Bib. 167, p. 95.
1928	Muratoff, Bib. 125, p. 144.		1946	Carli, Bib. 26, p. 25.
1928	Cecchi, Bib. 31, p. 14.		1948	Longhi, Bib. 100, p. 36.
1928	Weigelt, Bib. 195, p. 204, n.		1949	Garrison, Bib. 73, No. 376.
1929	Sandberg-Vavalà, Bib. 149, pp. 637, 809.		1950	Offner, Bib. 133, pp. 62, 65, 66.
1930	Weigelt, Bib. 194, p. 9.		1953	Sandberg-Vavalà, Bib. 153, pp. 51, 52, 53.
1931	Lasareff, Bib. 95, p. 166.			
1931	Weigelt, Bib. 193, pp. 21, 22.		1955	Carli, Bib. 28, pp. 30-32.
1932	Berenson, Bib. 15, p. 269.		1957	Stubblebine, Bib. 176, p. 34 n. 36.
1932	Edgell, Bib. 61, p. 34.		1958	Siena, Bib. 165, pp. 17-19.
1933	Siena, Bib. 164, pp. 110-11.		1959	Stubblebine, Bib. 175, p. 268.
1935	D'Ancona, Bib. 51, p. 89.		1961	DeWald, Bib. 59, pp. 80-81.

XX. *Montaione Madonna*

FIGURE 54   Montaione, San Regolo   H 165 x W 80 cm.

There is considerable repainting in the faces of the Madonna and the Child as well as the footstool. Parts, such as the throneback, have been rubbed. The gold background has been regilded.

This panel is not known in the literature, having come to light only recently.

The panel is certainly to be dated after the Palazzo Pubblico *Madonna*, that is, later than 1280. From that work are borrowed the cusped arch and the spandrel angels. As for the cusped arch, this has only a single molding, a feature of late Guidesque painting. It is also significant that the figure of the Madonna is of more slender proportions than in earlier Guidesque painting as can be seen especially in a comparison of the painting with the San Bernardino *Madonna* (Fig. 31). The tall, slender proportion of the entire panel and the steep pitch of the gable, so different from earlier panels of the Madonna Enthroned, are to be related to tendencies at the end of the century.

The absence of a headcloth on the Madonna is likewise a late feature and is the only instance of the omission in Guidesque representations of the Madonna Enthroned. The two most important *Madonnas* of the late thirteenth century come to mind here: Duccio's Rucellai *Madonna* (Fig. 125) and Cimabue's Trinita *Madonna* (Fig. 126), in both of which the dark mantle is similarly drawn up over the head. In this connection it is interesting to note that the Madonna's left hand is in the same position as in the Trinita *Madonna*.

The inclusion of the miniature figure of St. Michael, as in the case of the kneeling saints in the San Gimignano *Madonna* (Fig. 60) and the Krakow Tabernacle (Fig. 57), relates to developments of the late thirteenth century and the early fourteenth century. Finally, despite the extensive repainting in the faces of the Madonna and Child, something of the original can be found; thus the bridge of the nose of the Madonna has that shallow depression we find in early Ducciesque painting. Obviously, the Montaione *Madonna* is a fairly late work of the shop, executed at a point where the older formulas could be relaxed and where the painter was subjected to such newer influences as that of Duccio.

Garrison's suggestion of a relationship between this panel and the Memphis Polyptych (Figs. 50, 122) must be questioned on the grounds of the divergent concepts of form in the two. The knobby legs of the Child in the Polyptych as well as the hands of the other figures and the carved, wooden quality of their features have no counterpart in the Montaione painting. On the other hand, there are a number of points where the Montaione painting resembles the St. Peter Altarpiece (Fig. 53). The single molding of the cusped arch and the reversed perspective of the throne whereby both sides are shown may only reflect the contemporaneity of the two, but there is also a curious similarity in the paper-thin rendering of the parts of the thrones. The spandrel angels of the Montaione panel are remarkably close to those bland-faced creatures in the spandrels of the St. Peter panel and also the angel in the *Liberation of Peter from Prison* (Fig. 115). Difficult as it is at times to distinguish hands in Guido's shop and following, it is tempting to think that the St. Peter Master was responsible for the Montaione panel. In the handling of facial forms, in the inability to grasp the three-dimensional qualities of furniture, and in a susceptibility to the softer charms of Duccio, these two paintings betray strong affinities. Both give ample evidence of the artist's maturity and also of his independence from Guido; especially in this they differ from the earlier works we attribute to this hand, the Gallerani Shutters No. 5 (Figs. 35, 36) and the Grosseto *Last Judgment* (Fig. 49).

BIBLIOGRAPHY

1947 Garrison, Bib. 74, pp. 300, 303.   1949 Garrison, Bib. 73, No. 207.

LATER ASSISTANTS AND FOLLOWERS

XXI. *San Gimignano Crucifix.* APRON: *Virgin Mary* (L.), *St. John Evange-list* (R.); TERMINALS: *Two Prophets*; CIMASA: *Half-length Christ*

FIGURES 55, 121   San Gimignano, the Galleria del Palazzo Comunale No. 1   H 313 x W 248 cm.

There are scattered damages throughout, especially in the legs of Christ and in the right apron and terminal. There are conspicuous surface breaks such as that between the apron and the cross arms. There is no repaint, unless, as is possible, the crown of thorns be a later addition.

The previous history of the work is unknown.

This is the sole example of a painted cross in the Guidesque oeuvre. The presence of the Virgin and the Evangelist on either side in the apron of the Cross makes the representation an abbreviated Crucifixion scene. In this, the Cross differs from those containing scenes of the Passion in the apron; the two types run concurrently through thirteenth century Tuscan painting (Garrison, pp. 174-176, 181-182). Whereas the storied crosses were probably to be seen close up, a cross of the San Gimignano type with large figures could be hung at a greater height. The medallion of the half-length blessing Christ in the *cimasa* (Fig. 121) occurs in a great number of thirteenth century crosses and is to be interpreted as a highly abbreviated Ascension of Christ (Bib. 149, p. 171). The figure of Christ is stylistically derivative of that in Guido's Palazzo Pub-blico gable (Fig. 15): in the arrangement of the hands, in the draperies, and in the configurations of face and hair.

In the main field of the Cross the full-length Christ differs considerably from that in the *Crucifixion* (Fig. 116) from the Badia Ardenga and that in the Gallerani Shut-ters (Fig. 120). The dissimilarities from the latter two are thoroughgoing. For ex-ample, the pear-shaped abdomen has been abandoned so that the only strong torso definition remaining is the bow-shaped line of the pectorals. This evolvement away from bodily schematizations is a sign of the relative lateness of this rendition. The slump of the body of Christ is also at variance with the older formula of the pro-nounced arc of the torso. The same may be said of the position of the legs, the right being twisted over the left, so that both feet may be held by one nail. While the posture of the legs recalls that of the Christ figure on the Pisani Pulpit (Fig. 110) in the Siena Cathedral of the 1260's as well as the Giuntesque Cross in San Paolo a Ripa d'Arno, Pisa (*Giottesca*, fig. 17a), there are comparable examples late in the century such as the Cimabuesque Cross in the Fogg Museum (Garrison No. 465) and a Pisan example (Garrison No. 484).

This position of the legs may be a result of a misunderstanding of the new posture made popular by the generation of Duccio (Fig. 117) and Giotto, where the right foot of Christ is often placed over the left one. The difference is clearly observed in a comparison of two dated Crosses by Deodato Orlandi, those of 1288 (Fig. 118) and 1301 (Fig. 119). In the earlier one we see the exaggerated arching out of the torso and the overlapping of the left leg over the right which Cimabue used in the figure of the Crucified in the fresco (Fig. 89) at Assisi, and also found in the two Guidesque examples cited above, the scene from the Gallerani Shutters and the Badia Ardenga *Crucifixion*. In Deodato's later version of 1301, the limp body hangs straight down and the right foot is crossed over the left, in conformity with the new vogue. Our Guidesque Cross is much closer to the 1301 example than it is to the older fashion of Deodato's 1288 Crucifix.

Everything indicates that the Guidesque Cross was painted at a late point in the century when various new ideas are hesitantly taken up by followers of the older masters in Florence and Siena, followers, that is, of Cimabue and Guido. In a number of points of style a relation can be made to the Clarisse Master who painted the *Lord and Virgin Enthroned* (Fig. 123), and to whom we also attribute the Memphis Polyptych (Fig. 122) and the Krakow Tabernacle (Figs. 56-58). The nose of the Christ has the same hard, carved line we see in other works assigned to this artist. The handling of the *perizoma* recalls the drapery of the Child in the Memphis Polyptych. The rope-like strands of hair have the same peculiar effect as in his other works, and the moustache is the same, overly neat shape we see in the Lord of the Clarisse panel. The figures of the Virgin and St. John in the apron have the same shape and stance as the figures in the narrative scenes of the Krakow Tabernacle, while the prophets of the terminals are cousins, at least, of the flanking saints in the Memphis Polyptych. It is perhaps significant that in the Crucifixion scene (Fig. 58) of the Krakow Tabernacle, the right leg of Christ is placed in front of the left, exactly as in the painted Cross. This motif, as well as the stylistic parallels, suggest that the Cross is probably close in date to the Tabernacle. In comparison to the earlier works of the Clarisse Master, a date in the 1290's seems most reasonable for the Cross.

We cannot escape the conclusion that this assistant's work suffers the more he diverges from the Guidesque formula. The earliest work we have of his, the *Lord and Virgin Enthroned* of the 1270's, closely adheres to the modes of Guido and it is certainly his masterpiece. When he moves away from Guido, we discover that he is not completely self-sustaining.

BIBLIOGRAPHY

1929 Sandberg-Vavalà, Bib. 149, pp. 819-21.
1931 Chellini, Bib. 33, p. 40.
1935 D'Ancona, Bib. 51, pp. 97-98.
1937 Oertel, Bib. 130, p. 225.

1943 *Giottesca*, Bib. 167, pp. 100-101.
1948 Longhi, Bib. 100, p. 36.
1949 Garrison, Bib. 73, No. 490.

XXII. *Krakow Tabernacle: Madonna and Child Enthroned with Angels and Two Kneeling Saints*; SHUTTERS: *Crucifixion* (L.), *Entombment* (R.)

FIGURES 56, 57, 58   Krakow, National Museum, Czartoryski Collection,   H 34 x W (open) 42 cm.
No. V.235

There are extensive damages to many parts of the work as a result of flaking surfaces and much repainting. The Madonna's face had been gone over. The painting has recently been restored. The full-length saints on the exterior of the shutters are later and unrelated stylistically.

The history of the panel is unknown. Since the kneeling saints are most probably to be identified with St. Francis and St. Clare, the Tabernacle may have been in honor of St. Clare, possibly in a chapel dedicated to her.

The over-all shape is described as a gabled tabernacle with an inscribed arch. The form seems to be Sienese in origin (Garrison, pp. 130, 132-33). Other examples of this shape are the Tabernacle in the London National Gallery by Duccio (Fig. 128) and the one in the Boston Museum of Fine Arts by a follower (Bib. 20, fig. 107). The painter of the Krakow Tabernacle must have derived the form from the shop of Duccio where it seems to have been developed.

Another late motif is the curtain held by angels behind the Madonna. This too is apparently an invention of Duccio; it appears in his small *Madonna with Three Franciscans* of around 1280 (Fig. 127), and again in the later Tabernacle in the Fogg Museum (Bib. 20, figs. 13-14). The motif of kneeling supplicants, as in the San Gimignano *Madonna* (Fig. 60), is a feature we associate with the end of the thirteenth century and the beginning of the fourteenth. Altogether, the Krakow Tabernacle contains enough non-Guidesque elements to make one believe the painter of it was by that time out of the shop and free to borrow from the Ducciesque stock-in-trade.

Despite the late features there are certain archaisms that betray the older tradition in which this painter was trained. The flat, symmetrical throne with its tipped-up, two-dimensional seat is scarcely as evolved as those of Coppo in the 1260's. And, as Offner (Bib. 133) has pointed out, the Madonna is very close to Coppo's Orvieto *Madonna* (Fig. 81) in the complexity of her contrapposto position. The color, too, is strongly reminiscent of Coppo's warm tones. Finally, the white headcloth of the Madonna is anachronistic in a work containing so many late features.

The tarnished and in places illegible narratives on the shutters are also at some remove from the main stream of Guidesque narrative. A late date, probably in the 1290's, would go far to explain such divergence from the Guidesque manner as the angels flying above the cross in the scene of the Crucifixion. There are no previous examples of this motif in Sienese painting and it occurs nowhere else in the Guidesque oeuvre. It is, however, found in Cimabue's fresco (Fig. 89) in the upper church at Assisi as well as several works of the Magdalen Master.

101

The Christ figure in the Crucifixion scene has his right leg crossed over his left, a motif we find in the San Gimignano Crucifix (Fig. 55) and in the Yale *Crucifixion* (Fig. 52), both of which are less close to Guido and of later date than the typical Guidesque formulation seen in the Badia Ardenga *Crucifixion* and the Gallerani Shutters.

The attribution of this panel to the Clarisse Master (Bib. 73, Bib. 132, Bib. 133), author of the *Lord and Virgin Enthroned* (Fig. 34), the Memphis Polyptych (Fig. 50) and the San Gimignano Crucifix (Fig. 55), seems reasonable from every viewpoint.

As has been noted, the Krakow Tabernacle abounds in late features; besides, it exhibits a much looser drawing style. Whereas the throneback in the *Lord and Virgin Enthroned* describes a limited space, the space in the Krakow Madonna's compartment is to be aligned with a later period and the achievements of the younger Duccio. The postures and types of the Virgin and the Evangelist in the Crucifixion scene on the left shutter recall the same figures in the apron of the San Gimignano Cross, which we assign to the same decade. The degree to which this painting is removed from Guido is revealed as well as anything by the mountains in the *Entombment*; sparsely vegetated and of precipitous measure, they have none of the lustrous highlights that so distinguish Guido's own landscapes.

The Tabernacle, then, seems to be a product of the 1290's, at a time when the painter may no longer have been an assistant in the shop. Such an assistant, whose career can be traced with some accuracy, can provide considerable insight into the nature of, and changes in, the workshop of Guido.

BIBLIOGRAPHY

1914 Krakow, Bib. 92, No. 178.
1929 Krakow, Bib. 93, p. 10.
1947 Offner, Bib. 132, p. 7.
1949 Garrison, Bib. 73, p. 15 and No. 347.
1950 Offner, Bib. 133, pp. 72-73 n. 8.
1954 Shorr, Bib. 155, p. 32.
1957 Bialostocki, Bib. 18, pp. 463, 569.

XXIII. *Wellesley Tabernacle Center: The Funeral of St. Clare, The Mounting of the Cross*

FIGURE 59   Wellesley, Massachusetts, the Wellesley College Museum   H 79 x W 52 cm.

Only minute traces of the original silver ground remain. The panel was restored in 1957 at which time flaking paint was reset and the panel was fortified along the vertical fracture left of center. The cleaning revealed a good range of lustrous colors.

An inscription runs along the band between the two scenes:

[HIC] EST SEPULTURA BEATAE CLARAE INQUAE SANCTISSIM[US] PAPA [INNO-CENTUS] [A]S[TI]TIT CUM CARDINALIBUS [ET] FRATRIBUS MINORIBUS [ET] SORORIBUS [TERTII] ORDINIS

I am indebted to Morton C. Bradley and Dario Covi for the deciphering of this badly damaged inscription.

The panel was purchased for the Museum in 1905. It had previously been the property of the Marchesa Albergotti, Arezzo.

In over-all shape the Tabernacle must have followed the Sienese style in which arched shutters fit into the inscribed arch of the center panel (Garrison, Group XIII). A tabernacle without a central image does not occur before the end of the century; only then do we find such a work as the Tabernacle in the collection of the Earl of Crawford and Balcarres, London (Garrison No. 351) which gives over its central compartment to narrative. Thus, a Sienese origin and a fairly late date are indicated for the Wellesley panel, as in the case of the similar Tabernacle in Krakow (Fig. 56).

The combination of the two scenes with such contrasting themes is as curious as anything we find in the entire Guidesque oeuvre. Unfortunately, the inscription refers only to the funeral of St. Clare and does not, as we might hope, explain the juxtaposition of it with the *Mounting of the Cross* above. It tells how the funeral was attended by Pope Innocent IV with his court, by the Friars Minor, and the Sisters of the Third Order. We have quite a bit of information about the proceedings of the actual funeral from the life of St. Clare by Tomaso da Celano (Bib. 32, pp. 76-78). The author relates that when the Friars began to chant the Office of the Dead, the Pope interrupted, urging them to chant the Office of the Holy Virgins. This irregularity was, it seems, opposed by Bishop Rainaldo of Ostia, later Pope Alexander IV, and the Office of the Dead was resumed. Few incidents from the legend of the Saint convey more interest than that of her funeral. Left of center in our panel are the Friars Minor, one of whom gestures towards the Tertiary nuns who are distinguished from the Poor Clares by their white veils. Nearest the bier stands the Pope, while his cortege is gathered at the right. The Funeral of St. Clare in the Dossal in Santa Chiara, Assisi (Marle, I, fig. 227) of the 1280's has much the same arrangement.

The *Mounting of the Cross* in the upper half of the panel follows the representation of the same subject in the panel (Fig. 26) from the Badia Ardenga group. This is especially true of the figure of the Virgin, holding her Son by the waist and restraining the youth at the left. Such differences as there are appear to be simplifications of the model by Guido. Thus, in the Wellesley scene the lateral crosses are omitted, as is the architectural setting.

Nothing in the accounts of St. Clare's life explicitly justifies the inclusion of this scene from the Passion of Christ. But we know from Celano of the Saint's devotion to the Cross and to the "delizie del Crocifisso," and that St. Francis sent afflicted persons to her to be cured by the sign of the cross (Bib. 32, pp. 52-53, 56). St. Clare, like St. Francis, is often associated with the cross. In the Dossal in Santa Chiara, Assisi, she carries a cross in her left hand and points to it with her right. And in the Crucifix of the 1260's, also in Santa Chiara, she kneels at the feet of the Crucified

(Bib. 149, figs. 528-29). An order of Tertiaries commissioning such a tabernacle might very well have thought of an episode connected with the cross. The very imaginative scene of the Mounting of the Cross in Guido's San Domenico Altarpiece may have seemed a very appropriate one to borrow. The program of the shutters may have included full-length saints, or narratives, or a combination of the two. If narratives, we might expect to find the Expulsion of the Saracens on the left and the Crucifixion on the right.

The painter was very probably a provincial, as is indicated by the strangely accentuated schematizations of nose and brow. It is difficult to estimate what relation he may have had with the shop of Guido: he is neither less gifted nor more remote than several of the assistants who seem to have worked on certain parts of the Badia Ardenga narratives. The face of the Virgin resembles those of certain secondary figures in that group. The use of black daubs between the lips, under the nasal wing, and for the pupil of the eye is a simplification of the Guidesque scheme, used for example in the three Marys of the *Entombment* (Fig. 30). Whatever his shortcomings, this artist can charm with rhythmic groupings and with a vibrant color which the recent cleaning has revealed.

As we have noted, the panel shape itself provides evidence for a date late in the century. The derivation of the scene of the Mounting of the Cross certainly precludes a date earlier than the 1280's. Given the tenuous relationship of the painter to the shop and the probability that he worked away from the shop, we may date the panel in the 1290's or later.

BIBLIOGRAPHY

1929   Sandberg-Vavalà, Bib. 149, p. 280.   1958   Wellesley, Bib. 196, pp. 64-67.
1949   Garrison, Bib. 73, No. 342.

XXIV. *San Gimignano Madonna*

FIGURE 60   San Gimignano, the Galleria del Palazzo Comunale   H 170 x W 134 cm.

Most of the gable was cut off as well as a strip along the bottom at the time of a refurbishing in 1699. At that time the entire panel was repainted with the exception of the heads of the Madonna and Child (illustrated Bib. 27, fig. 3). The panel was restored in 1949. The surface had been badly scraped at the time of the repainting; some surfaces were found to be completely erased. The three angels in the right spandrel are fairly well-preserved; the kneeling saints in the lower part of the picture are very damaged. In eking out the gable to its original form, the restorers chose to paint in the general shapes of the Redeemer and angels.

The panel came from Sant'Agostino in San Gimignano; Brogi (Bib. 24) saw it in the Sacristy of that Church in 1865. Carli (Bib. 27) supposes the painting went from Siena to San Gimignano with a migration of Augustinians in 1272. Their church in San Gimignano was only begun in 1280 and not consecrated until 1298. Since the painting is a late work, it was indubitably made for the San Gimignano church, perhaps soon after the consecration of 1298.

The connection with the Augustinian Order is confirmed by the presence of two members of that Order in the kneeling figures. The saint on the left is St. Augustine and that on the right is the Beata Giuliana Corneliense (1193-1259), identified by the Augustinian nun's habit, a white tunic with a dark mantle and a white wimple over the black veil.

With the exception of the unstriated white headcloth of the Madonna falling to a point on her breast, no feature of this painting reasonably aligns it with the early Guidesque Madonna Enthroned formula exemplified by the San Bernardino and Arezzo *Madonnas* (Figs. 31, 32). Even the gesture of the Child seems less like the blessing motion of the Child in the early Guidesque type of Madonna and rather more like a pale imitation of the Child reaching for his mother's veil, a motif which originates with Duccio, as in the Tabernacle (Fig. 128) in the London National Gallery. The way the legs of the Child are spread apart rather than crossed is not paralleled in Guidesque paintings but is, once again, a weak reflection of that vigorous posture employed by Duccio for the Child in the *Madonna with Three Franciscans* (Fig. 127) and in the Rucellai *Madonna* (Fig. 125).

The foregoing points alone might be enough to upset Carli's belief that this is an early *Madonna* by Guido and that it offers a prototype and precedent for the Palazzo Pubblico *Madonna*. A number of the advanced features are less anticipations than they are simplifications. The cusped arch is now painted instead of being in relief. Certainly the fact that the gable is not separated from the Madonna panel by a complex of relief moldings is a matter of simplification. The addition of the slender colonnettes and capitals is an attempt to give Guido's decorative cusped arch some sort of rational function. It is a curious fact that such supporting colonnettes are a relatively late feature in Sienese Dugento painting: aside from the problematical St. John Altarpiece in the Siena Pinacoteca, the earliest example of it in Sienese painting is the Madonna del Voto Polyptych as reconstructed here (Fig. 38). It will appear again in the St. Francis Altarpiece of the early fourteenth century (Fig. 61).

The angels hovering above the cusped arch originated, not here certainly, but in the Palazzo Pubblico *Madonna*. In fact, they are closer in the San Gimignano *Madonna* to the arrangement in works by Duccio, such as the London Tabernacle mentioned above, where the figures are more diminutive and shown in fuller length. Whereas all the other Madonnas in the Guidesque oeuvre have a throneback decorated with disks, the San Gimignano panel has a throneback decorated with interlacing polygons in the manner of the throneback in Duccio's Rucellai *Madonna*.

Most significant is the presence of the two kneeling saints at the feet of the Madonna. That this is a practice more common to the early fourteenth century has already been noted. The only thirteenth century Sienese equivalents are the monks in the *Madonna with Three Franciscans* of about 1280, an early work by Duccio, and the saints in the late Krakow Tabernacle (Fig. 57), which is strongly influenced by Ducciesque ideas.

The connection with the new style of Duccio can be detected in other ways. The position of the left hand of the San Gimignano Madonna indicates an interest in the Rucellai *Madonna* (Fig. 125). The placing of hand and fingers is closer to that than to the artful gesture in the Palazzo Pubblico *Madonna* (Fig. 14). The gentle curve of the nose, the drawing of the nasal wing, and, above all, the smoothing and flattening of the bridge of the nose are similar to the treatment of those features in the Rucellai *Madonna* and in the Ducciesque *Madonna* in Crevole (Marle, II, fig. 2). There is, furthermore, a reduction in the intensity and amount of highlighting on the face so that it takes on a gentler and more natural expression.

Undeniably the panel is of good quality and the figures, as the angels in the right spandrel, have a muted charm. They are not, however, equals to the passionate, vivacious angels (Fig. 17) in the spandrels of the Palazzo Pubblico *Madonna*. It would be difficult to defend the San Gimignano *Madonna* as a work by Guido himself. Perhaps it is the mistaken belief that this is a work by Guido which encourages Carli to think of the artist as working out the problems of the Palazzo Pubblico painting in this work.

Everything indicates that we are confronted with a painter who was Guidesque in training but much influenced by the new art of Duccio. The figure style of this painting reflects that of the Rucellai *Madonna* of 1285. Other features, such as the kneeling saints and the light tonality of the throne, similar to the marble inlay of the mature Duccio and his school, urge a still later date of around 1300. The marvel, then, is that the Palazzo Pubblico *Madonna* by Guido should have exerted such an influence for so long a period of time. It is possible that the painter of the San Gimignano *Madonna* made it at a time when the San Domenico Altarpiece had been dismembered and the refurbished *Madonna* together with the pediment were hung in another part of San Domenico.

BIBLIOGRAPHY

1865	Brogi, Bib. 24 (pub. 1897), p. 502.	1955	Carli, Bib. 27, pp. 15-33.
1923	Marle, Bib. 107, I, p. 368.	1955	Carli, Bib. 28, p. 24 n.
1932	Perkins, Bib. 139, p. 87.	1955	Carli, Bib. 29, pp. 176-78.
1949	Garrison, Bib. 73, No. 34.	1959	Stubblebine, Bib. 175, p. 268.
1951	Brandi, Bib. 20, p. 115.		

XXV. *St. Francis Altarpiece.* CENTER: *St. Francis.* LATERAL NARRATIVES (clockwise from lower left) : *The Saint Giving Up His Clothes, The Miracle in San Damiano, The Dream of Innocent III, The Sermon to the Birds, The Fiery Chariot, The Stigmatization, The Miracle at Greccio, The Funeral of the Saint.* GABLE: *Redeemer and Eight Angels*

FIGURE 61   Siena Pinacoteca No. 313   H 232 x W 113 cm.

The panel had been much repainted; in the 1931 restoration the later stigmata and the multifoil decorations were removed. Surfaces are still much damaged. There is a vertical split at the bottom to the right of the central figure. The frame is original.

On the dark ground between the feet of the Saint can be read the inscription, possibly repainted: · $\bar{s}$ · FRAC̄ISCUS

The picture came to the Siena Pinacoteca in 1871 from the Church of San Francesco in Colle di Val d'Elsa. It is listed as No. 15 in the 1895 Catalogue, and as No. 303 in the 1872 Catalogue.

This panel is the Guidesque interpretation of a popular thirteenth century subject in its typical form: a gabled dossal representing a full-length, standing St. Francis flanked by scenes from his legend. The examples (Garrison, Group XXII, pp. 154-56) begin with Bonaventura Berlinghieri's important panel in San Francesco, Pescia, dated 1235 (Fig. 62).

The panel shape itself provides conclusive proof of the lateness of this work. It is much taller and more slender than other gabled St. Francis panels, the nearest in proportion being the Santa Croce example (Fig. 124) in Florence where, however, a horizontal feeling is effected by the breadth of the scenes. The dominant verticality of the Guidesque St. Francis panel, taken together with the soaring, narrow arch moldings, proclaims a date well into the fourteenth century.

The figure of St. Francis is held in rigid frontality, as is customary for these rather hieratic representations of the Saint. This pose matches ill with the soft foldings of the drapery which are characteristic of the later age in which the panel was painted. It lacks the unity of the Santa Croce *St. Francis* where the frontality of the figure is complemented by the stylized draperies. The stylistic features of the Siena panel are essentially Guidesque, though now much modified with the passage of time and the advent of a newer style of painting.

It is significant that St. Francis holds a cross in his right hand. While this motif occurs only occasionally in images of the Saint by Margaritone and not at all in the thirteenth century historiated St. Francis panels, it is an important feature of the picture which the St. Francis Master painted on the supposed bed-pallet of St. Francis, in Santa Maria degli Angeli, Assisi (Fig. 105). This must have been an authoritative and venerated image and it gives further probability to the notion, discussed below, that the Guidesque painter of our panel had been in Assisi.

We may begin to realize how far this panel is removed from the formula of Guido's shop in its heyday when we look at the decoration of the halo, consisting of flower patterns set into little rectangles, a type which can be found nowhere else in the Guidesque ambient.

The grouping of the Redeemer and angels above the moldings at the top may be said to have its source in the spandrels and gable of the Palazzo Pubblico *Madonna*. However, in the more diminutive size and the greater length of the figures, this arrangement is abreast of Duccio's Old Testament figures in the gable of his Tabernacle (Fig. 128) in the London National Gallery of the beginning of the fourteenth century.

The late date of the narratives in the side fields can be demonstrated both stylistically and iconographically. In the *Miracle in San Damiano*, the extreme slenderness of the figure of the Crucified and the absence of any strong arching of the torso relate the figure to such early fourteenth century examples as that in the Crucifix (Fig. 119) by Deodato Orlandi dated 1301, rather than such an earlier Guidesque example as the *Crucifixion* (Fig. 116) from the Badia Ardenga group.

Above all, the iconographic program of these narratives removes this Altarpiece from the St. Francis panels of the thirteenth century. All of these—in Pescia, Pisa, Pistoia, Florence, the lost one from San Miniato (Garrison Nos. 402, 408, 409, 405, 410), as well as two rectangular ones in Assisi and Rome (Garrison Nos. 361, 371)—have actually only three scenes from the legend of the Saint in common. These are the Healing of the Child, the Healing of Bartolommeo da Narni, and the Healing of the Possessed. Strikingly, none of these scenes are to be found in the Siena *St. Francis*. On the other hand, every one of the episodes in the Siena panel is to be found in the fresco series of the life of St. Francis in the upper church at Assisi. And, in fact, four of these scenes occur nowhere else before the Assisi frescoes: the Miracle in San Damiano, the Dream of Innocent III, the Fiery Chariot, and the Funeral of the Saint. The lateness of the Siena panel can therefore be established not only by the remoteness from the usual program of the thirteenth century representations but also by the dependence on the fresco cycle in Assisi.

It is curious that in no case does the scene in the Siena *St. Francis* imitate the composition of the Assisi counterpart; rather, each scene is recast into a more familiar Guidesque mold. Thus, the *Stigmatization* recalls the representation in the early Shutters (Fig. 101) by Guido himself, and not, it is noteworthy, the Gallerani Shutters by the St. Peter Master. In one detail the scene differs from Guido's; there were apparently no rays between the angel and the Saint. During the modern restoration five rays which had been added later were removed. Guido's *Stigmatization* is also the reference for the kneeling Saint in the *Miracle in San Damiano*. In most instances the architecture follows the Guidesque formula, as in the *Miracle in San Damiano*, the *Stigmatization*, and the *Funeral of the Saint*. On the other hand, the loggias in the *Dream of Innocent III* and the *Giving up of the Clothes* are of a sophistication unknown to Guido and clearly of a later time. Recent criticism (Bib. 197, Bib. 116) has found rather definite evidence that the Assisi frescoes are datable to the first decade of the fourteenth century. There can be little question, then, that our Guidesque work dates from towards the end of that decade.

Critics have usually done little more than assign the painting to a late part of the thirteenth century and to a follower of Guido. He can hardly be the painter of the Shutters Nos. 4 and 5 as Toesca (Bib. 182) would have it. In fact, it is not possible to connect this painter with any other work in the Guidesque oeuvre. There can be no doubt that when this Altarpiece was painted the shop of Guido had been disbanded for some time. This *St. Francis* is chiefly interesting as a demonstration of the way in which Guidesque formulas continued into the new century, even to the point of transforming the modern style of Assisi into a Dugento idiom.

BIBLIOGRAPHY

1859 Biadi, Bib. 17, p. 306.
1865 Brogi, Bib. 24 (pub. 1897), p. 156.
1872 Siena, Bib. 159, p. 54.
1885 Thode, Bib. 178, pp. 90, 110, 115-16, 124, 139, 150.
1895 Siena, Bib. 160, p. 103.
1903 Siena, Bib. 161, p. 105.
1909 Siena, Bib. 162, p. 107.
1911 Weigelt, Bib. 191, p. 152.

1923 Marle, Bib. 107, I, p. 373.
1926 Bughetti, Bib. 25, pp. 67-72.
1927 Toesca, Bib. 182, I, p. 1038 n. 44.
1933 Siena, Bib. 164, pp. 119-20.
1939 Bacci, Bib. 7, p. 30.
1949 Garrison, Bib. 73, No. 411.
1953 Sandberg-Vavalà, Bib. 153, p. 49.
1956 White, Bib. 197, p. 347.
1958 Siena, Bib. 165, p. 14.

BIBLIOGRAPHY

1. Acta Sanctorum. "De B. Andrea de Galleranis Senis in Hetruria," *Acta Sanctorum quotquot toto orbe vel a Catholicis scriptoribus celebrantur* . . . , VIII, Martii, III, Antwerp, 1668, pp. 49-57.

2. Altenburg, Herzoglich Sachsen-Altenburgisches Museum. *Beschreibender Katalog der Gemaeldesammlung*, Altenburg, 1898.

3. Altenburg. *Italienische Malerei der vor- und Fruehrenaissance im Staatlichen Lindenau-Museum Altenburg*, Altenburg, 1952.

4. Arezzo, Pinacoteca. *La Pinacoteca di Arezzo*, ed. A. Vita, Florence, 1921.

5. Arezzo, Pinacoteca. *Catalogo dell' Pinacoteca comunale di Arezzo*, ed. M. Salmi, Città di Castello, 1921.

6. Bacci, P. "Coppo di Marcovaldo e Salerno di Coppo," *L'Arte*, III, 1900, pp. 32-40.

7. Bacci, P. *Dipinti inediti e sconosciuti di Pietro Lorenzetti, Bernardo Daddi, ecc. in Siena e nel contado*, Siena, 1939.

8. Bacci, P. *Documenti toscani per la storia dell' arte*, Florence, 1910-12, 2 vols.

9. Bacci, P. "L'elenco delle pitture, sculture e architettura di Siena compilato nel 1625-26 da Mons. Fabio Chigi poi Alessandro VII secondo il ms. Chigiano I.i.11," *Bullettino senese di storia patria*, n.s. x, 1939, pp. 197-213, 297-337.

10. Bacci, P. "La R. Pinacoteca di Siena," *Bollettino d'arte*, XXVI, 1932, pp. 177-200.

11. Bacci, P. "La R. Pinacoteca di Siena," *Bullettino senese di storia patria*, n.s. IV, 1933, pp. 1-24.

12. Baldinucci, F. *Notizie de' professori del disegno da Cimabue in qua*, Florence, 1681 (ed. of 1811, Milan).

13. Barbi, F. *Vita del B. Andrea Gallerani*, Siena, 1638.

14. Beenken, H. "Notizen und Nachrichten, Italien, 13. und 14. Jahrhundert," *Zeitschrift fuer Kunstgeschichte*, II, 1933, pp. 132-34.

15. Berenson, B. *Italian Pictures of the Renaissance*, Oxford, 1932.

16. Berenson, B. "A Newly Discovered Cimabue," *Art in America*, VIII, 1920, pp. 260-61.

17. Biadi, L. *Storia della città di Colle*, Florence, 1859.

18. Bialostocki, J. and Walicki, M. *Europaeische Malerei in Polnischen Sammlungen*, Warsaw, 1957.

19. Bonaventura, St. *Doctoris Seraphici S. Bonaventurae S.R.E. Episcopi Cardinalis Omnia Opera* . . . ed. Quaracchi (Florence), 10 vols., 1882-1902.

20. Brandi, C. *Duccio*, Florence, 1951.

21. Brandi, C. "Una Madonna del 1262 ed ancora il problema di Guido da Siena," *L'Arte*, XXXVI, 1933, pp. 3-13.

22. Brandi, C. "A proposito di una felice ricostruzione della celebre Madonna di Guido da Siena," *Bullettino senese di storia patria*, n.s. II, 1931, pp. 77-80.

23. Brandi, C. (and E. Carli). "Relazione sul restauro della Madonna di Guido da Siena del 1221," *Bollettino d'arte*, XXXVI, 1951, pp. 248-60.

24. Brogi, F. *Inventario generale degli oggetti d'arte della provincia di Siena*, Siena, 1897 (compiled 1862-65).

25. Bughetti, B. *Vita e miracoli di S. Francesco nella tavole istoriate dei secoli XIII e XIV*, Quaracchi (Florence), 1926.

26. Carli, E. *Capolavori dell' arte senese*, Florence, 1946.

27. Carli, E. *Dipinti senesi del contado e della Maremma*, Milan, 1955.

28. Carli, E. *La pittura senese*, Milan, 1955.

29. Carli, E. "Recent Discoveries in Sienese Painting of the Thirteenth and Fourteenth Centuries," *The Connoisseur*, CXXXVI, 1955, pp. 176-78.

... Carli, E. "Relazione sul restauro della Madonna di Guido . . . ," see Brandi, Bib. 23.

30. Carli, E. *Vetrata duccesca*, Florence, 1946.

31. Cecchi, E. *I trecentisti senesi*, Rome, 1928.

32. Celano, Tomaso da. *La Leggenda di Santa Chiara d'Assisi, cavata dal codice magliabecchiano . . .*, ed. G. Battelli, n.p., 1952.

33. Chellini, L. *Guida storico-artistica di San Gimignano*, Florence, 1931.

34. Coletti, L. "La Mostra Giottesca," *Bollettino d'arte*, s. 3, xv, 1937, pp. 49-72.

35. Coletti, L. *I primitivi*, Novaro, 1941-47, 3 vols.

36. Cologne. *Catalogue des collections d'objets d'art de Mr. Jean Ant. Ramboux, vente publique à Cologne le 23 mai, 1867*, J. M. Heberle (ed.), Cologne, 1867.

37. Cologne. *Verzeichnis der Gemaelde-Sammlung des Museums Wallraf-Richartz*, Cologne, 1888.

38. Coor, G. "Coppo di Marcovaldo, his Art in Relation to the Art of his Time," *Marsyas*, v, 1949, pp. 1-21.

39. Coor, G. "Ducento-Gemaelde aus der Sammlung Ramboux," *Wallraf-Richartz Jahrbuch*, xvi, 1954, pp. 77-86.

40. Coor, G. "The Earliest Italian Representation of the Coronation of the Virgin," *Burlington Magazine*, xcix, 1957, pp. 328-330.

41. Coor, G. "An Early Italian Tabernacle," *Gazette des Beaux-Arts*, 6 ser. xxvi, 1944, pp. 129-52.

42. Coor, G. "A Neglected Work by the Magdalen Master," *Burlington Magazine*, lxxxix, 1947, pp. 119-29.

43. Coor, G. "Notes on Two Unknown Early Italian Panel Paintings," *Gazette des Beaux-Arts*, 6 ser. xlii, 1953, pp. 257-58.

44. Coor, G. "Some Unknown Representations by the Magdalen Master," *Burlington Magazine*, xciii, 1951, pp. 73-78.

45. Coor, G. "A Visual Basis for the Documents Relating to Coppo di Marcovaldo and his Son Salerno," *Art Bulletin*, xxviii, 1946, pp. 233-47.

46. Crowe, J. A. and Cavalcaselle, G. B. *A New History of Painting in Italy from the Second to the Sixteenth Century*, London, 1864, 3 vols.

47. Cruttwell, M. *A Guide to the Paintings in the Florentine Galleries . . .*, London and New York, 1907.

48. Dalton, O. M. *Byzantine Art and Archeology*, Oxford, 1911.

49. Dami, L. *Siena e le sue opere d'arte*, Florence, 1915.

50. Da Morrona, A. *Pisa illustrata*, 1792 (2nd ed., Pisa, 1812).

51. D'Ancona, P. *Les primitifs italiens du XIe au XIIIe siècle*, Paris, 1935.

52. David, E. *Histoire de la Peinture au moyen âge*, Paris, 1863.

53. Davidsohn, R. "Guido von Siena," *Repertorium fuer Kunstwissenschaft*, xxix, 1906, pp. 262-67.

54. Davidsohn, R. "Guido von Siena," *Repertorium fuer Kunstwissenschaft*, xxx, 1907, p. 383.

55. De Angelis, L. *Ragguaglio del nuovo istituto delle belle arti stabilito in Siena . . . quadri dell' antica scuola sanese . . .*, Siena, 1816.

56. Della Valle, Padre G. *Lettere senesi di un socio dell' accademia di Fossano sopra le belle arti*, Venice and Rome, 1782-86, 3 vols.

57. De Nicola, G. *Mostra di opere di Duccio di Buoninsegna e della sua scuola*, Siena, 1912.

58. De Nicola, G. Review of Weigelt, *Duccio, Bollettino senese di storia patria*, xviii, 1911, pp. 433-35.

59. DeWald, E. *Italian Painting 1200-1600*, New York, 1961.

60. Douglas, L. in *A History of Painting in Italy . . . by J. A. Crowe and G. B. Cavalcaselle*, ed. L. Douglas and T. Borenius, London, 1903-14, 6 vols.

61. Edgell, G. *A History of Sienese Painting*, New York, 1932.

62. Emerson, G. "The Kress Collection: a Gift to the Nation," *National Geographic*, cxx, No. 6, 1961, pp. 823-65.

63. Falciai, M. *Arezzo. La sua storia e i suoi monumenti*, Arezzo, 1925.

64. Faluschi, G. *Breve relazione delle cose notabili della città di Siena*, Siena, 1784.

65. Fisher, M. R. "Assisi, Padua, and the Boy in the Tree," *Art Bulletin*, XXXVIII, 1956, pp. 47-52.

66. Florence, R. Galleria dell' Accademia. *Elenco dei principali oggetti d'arte*, Florence, 1925.

67. Florence, R. Galleria dell' Accademia. *Elenco dei principali oggetti d'arte*, Florence, 1928.

68. Florence. Academy Gallery. *Catalogue of the Principal Paintings*, Florence, 1932.

69. Florence. *La R. Galleria dell' accademia di Firenze*, ed. U. Procacci, Rome, 1936.

70. Florence. *The Gallery of the Academy of Florence*, ed. U. Procacci, Rome, 1951.

71. Franchi, A. "Di alcuni recenti acquisti della Pinacoteca di Belle Arti in Siena," *Rassegna d'arte senese*, II, 1906, pp. 116-17.

72. Garrison, E. B. "A Berlinghieresque Fresco in S. Stefano, Bologna," *Art Bulletin*, XXVIII, 1946, pp. 211-32.

73. Garrison, E. B. *Italian Romanesque Panel Painting, an Illustrated Index*, Florence, 1949.

74. Garrison, E. B. "Post-War Discoveries. Early Italian Paintings. IV," *Burlington Magazine*, LXXXIX, 1947, pp. 299-303.

75. Garrison, E. B. "Sienese Historical Writings and the Dates 1260, 1221, and 1262 Applied to Sienese Paintings," *Studies in the History of Medieval Italian Painting*, IV, 1960, pp. 23-58.

76. Garrison, E. B. "Simeone and Machilone Spoletenses," *Gazette des Beaux-Arts*, 6 ser. XXXV, 1949, pp. 53-58.

77. Garrison, E. B. "Toward a New History of Early Lucchese Painting," *Art Bulletin*, XXXIII, 1951, pp. 11-31.

78. Garrison, E. B. "Toward a New History of the Siena Cathedral Madonnas," *Studies in the History of Medieval Italian Painting*, IV, 1960, pp. 5-22.

79. Gigli, Girolamo. *La città diletta di Maria, ovvero notizie istoriche appartenenti all' antica denominazione, che ha Siena di città della Vergine*, Rome, 1716.

80. Gigli, Girolamo. *Diario sanese*, Lucca, 1723, 2 vols. (2nd ed., Siena, 1854)

... *Giottesca*, see Sinibaldi, Bib. 167.

81. Harvard University, Fogg Art Museum. *Collection of Medieval and Renaissance Paintings*, Cambridge, 1919.

82. Harvard University, Fogg Art Museum. *Handbook*, Cambridge, 1927.

83. Harvard University, Fogg Art Museum. *Handbook*, Cambridge, 1936.

84. Heywood, W. and Olcott, L. *Guide to Siena, History and Art*, Siena, 1903.

85. Jacobsen, E. *Sienesische Meister des Trecento in der Gemaeldegalerie zu Siena*, Strasbourg, 1907.

86. Jansen, A. "Une peinture étrange," *Revue de l'art chrétien*, XXXVIII, 1888, pp. 281-86.

87. Jansen, A. in *Revue de l'art chrétien*, XXXIX, 1889, pp. 84-85.

88. Jarves, J. J. *Art Studies: the "Old Masters" of Italy; Paintings*, New York, 1861.

89. Jarves, J. J. *Descriptive Catalogue of the Paintings now on Exhibition at the Institute of Fine Arts* [Derby Gallery] ... *and the Unique Jarves Coll. of Old Masters*, New York, 1861.

90. Kaftal, G. *Iconography of the Saints in Tuscan Painting*, Florence, 1952.

91. Kaftal, G. *St. Dominic in Early Tuscan Painting*, Oxford, 1948.

92. Krakow, Czartoryski Museum. *Wydawnictwa Muzeum Czartoryskich, I. Galeria obrazow. Katalog tymczasowy*, Krakow, 1914.

93. Krakow, Czartoryski Museum. *Muzeum Książąt Czartoryskich w Krakowie*, ed. S. Komornicki, Krakow, 1929.

94. Lanzi, L. *Storia pittorica della Italia* . . . , Pisa, 1815-16, 6 vols.

95. Lasareff, V. "Duccio and Thirteenth Century Greek Icons," *Burlington Magazine*, LIX, 1931, pp. 154-69.

96. Lisini, A. "Una interessante questione artistica," *Miscellanea storica senese*, III, 1895, pp. 10-12.

97. Lisini, A. "Madonna degli occhi grossi," *Miscellanea storica senese*, I, 1893, pp. 10-11.

98. London. University. Courtauld Institute of Art. *Courtauld Institute Galleries Catalogue*, London, 1960.

99. London. University. Courtauld Institute of Art. *The Lee Collection*, London, 1959.

100. Longhi, R. "Giudizio sul duecento," *Proporzioni*, II, 1948, pp. 5-54.

101. Lusini, V. *Il duomo di Siena*, Siena, 1911-39, 2 vols.

102. Lusini, V. "Mostra Ducciana. Catalogo dei dipinti," *Rassegna d'arte senese*, VIII, 1912, pp. 105-54.

103. Lusini, V. "San Domenico in Camporegio," *Bullettino senese di storia patria*, o.s. XXII, 1906, pp. 263-95.

104. Mamachi, Tommaso M. *Annalium ordinis praedicatorum . . .* , Rome, 1756.

105. Mancini, G. *Considerazione sulla pittura pubblicate per la prima volta da Adriana Marucchi*, ed. L. Salerno, Rome, 1956-57, 2 vols.

106. Mandonnet, P. *St. Dominic and his Work*, St. Louis, 1948.

107. Marle, R. van. *The Development of the Italian Schools of Painting*, The Hague, 1923-38, 19 vols.

108. Marle, R. van. "Dipinti senesi nel museo arcivescovile di Utrecht," *Bollettino d'arte*, n.s. II, 1923, pp. 529-69.

109. Marle, R. van, ed. *Gemme d'arte antica italiana . . .* , Milan, 1938.

110. Marle, R. van. "La pittura senese prima di Duccio," *Rassegna d'arte antica e moderna*, VII, 1920, pp. 265-73.

111. Marle, R. van. *Recherches sur l'iconographie de Giotto et de Duccio*, Strasbourg, 1920.

112. Marle, R. van. "La scuola di Pietro Cavallini a Rimini," *Bollettino d'arte*, XV, 1921, pp. 248-61.

113. Mather, F. J. *A History of Italian Painting*, New York, 1923.

114. Mather, F. J. "Painting," *Art and Archaeology, the Arts Throughout the Ages*, XX, No. 3, 1925, pp. 145-51.

115. Meiss, M. "A Dugento Altarpiece at Antwerp," *Burlington Magazine*, LXXI, 1937, pp. 14-24.

116. Meiss, M. *Giotto and Assisi*, New York, 1960.

117. Meiss, M. "A New Early Duccio," *Art Bulletin*, XXXIII, 1951, pp. 95-103.

118. Meiss, M. *Painting in Florence and Siena after the Black Death*, Princeton, 1951.

119. Memphis, Brooks Memorial Art Gallery. *The Samuel H. Kress Collection*, ed. W. Suida, Memphis, 1958.

120. Milanesi, G. "Della vera età di Guido pittore senese e della celebre sua tavola in San Domenico di Siena," *Giornale storia degli archivi toscani*, III, 1859, pp. 3-13. Reprinted and more accessible in Idem, *Sulla storia dell' arte toscana, scritti varj*, Siena, 1873, pp. 89-103.

121. Millet, G. *Recherches sur l'iconographie de l'évangile aux XIVe, XVe, et XVIe siècles . . .* , Paris, 1916.

122. Montault, B. de. "L'influence de Saint Bonaventure sur l'art italien à propos des peintures d'Utrecht et de Florence," *Revue de l'art chrétien*, XXIX, 1889, pp. 84-85.

123. Montfaucon, B. de. *Diarium italicum, sive monumentorum veterum, Bibliothecarum, Musaeorum, etc. Notitiae singulares in Itinere Italico collectae*, Paris, 1702.

124. Montfaucon, B. de. *L'Etruria pittrice*, Florence, 1791.

125. Muratoff, P. *La peinture byzantine*, Rome, 1928.

126. Muratori. *Rerum italicarum scriptores . . .* , Città di Castello, 1900-55, 34 vols.

127. Nicolosi, C. *Il litorale maremmano*, Bergamo, 1910.

128. Oertel, R. *Fruehe italienische Malerei in Altenburg*, Berlin, 1961.

129. Oertel, R. *Fruehzeit der italienischen Malerei*, Stuttgart, 1953.

130. Oertel, R. "Giotto-Ausstellung in Florenz," *Zeitschrift fuer Kunstgeschichte*, VI, 1937, pp. 218-38.

113

131. Oertel, R. "Italienische Malerei des Mittelalters bis zum Trecento," *Zeitschrift fuer Kunstgeschichte*, VII, 1938, pp. 263-67.

132. Offner, R. *A Critical and Historical Corpus of Florentine Painting*, New York, 1930-60, 9 vols.

133. Offner, R. "Guido da Siena and A.D. 1221," *Gazette des Beaux-Arts*, 6 ser. XXXVII, 1950, pp. 61-90.

134. Offner, R. *Italian Primitives at Yale University: Comments and Revisions*, New Haven, 1927.

135. Offner, R. "Note on an Unknown St. Francis in the Louvre," *Gazette des Beaux-Arts*, 6 ser. XXXIX, 1952, pp. 129-33.

136. Ostoia, V. K. "A Palmesel at the Cloisters," *The Metropolitan Museum of Art Bulletin*, XIV, 1956, pp. 170-73.

137. Pecci, G. A. *Relazione delle cose più notabili della città di Siena*, Siena, 1752.

138. Perkins, F. M. "Dipinti senesi sconosciuti o inediti," *Rassegna d'arte*, XIV, 1914, pp. 97-104.

139. Perkins, F. M. "Pitture senesi poco conosciute," *La Diana*, VII, 1932, pp. 79-90.

140. Quétif, J. and Echard, P., eds. *Scriptores ordinis praedicatorum*, Paris, 1719.

141. Rankin, W. *Notes on the Collections of Old Masters at Yale University*, Wellesley, 1905.

142. Richard, Abbé. *Description historique et critique de l'Italie, ou nouveaux mémoires*, Paris, 1770, 3 vols.

143. Romagnoli, E. *Cenni storico-artistici di Siena e suoi suburbii*, Siena, O. Porri (ed.), 1840.

144. Rosini, G. *Storia della pittura italiana esposta coi monumenti*, Pisa, 1839-1855, 9 vols.

145. Rothes, W. *Die Bluetezeit der sienesischen Malerei und ihre Bedeutung fuer die Entwicklung der italienischen Kunst*, Strasbourg, 1904.

146. Rumohr, K. F. Z. P. von. *Italienische Forschungen*, Berlin and Stettin, 1827.

147. Salmi, M. *L'Arte italiana*. I. (*Dalle origini cristiane a tutto il periodo romanico*), Florence, 1943.

148. Salmi, M. "La mostra Giottesca," *Emporium*, LXXXVI, 1937, pp. 349-64.

149. Sandberg-Vavalà, E. *La croce dipinta e l'iconografia della passione*, Verona, 1929.

150. Sandberg-Vavalà, E. *L'iconografia della Madonna*, Siena, 1934.

151. Sandberg-Vavalà, E. "The Madonnas of Guido da Siena," *Burlington Magazine*, LXIV, 1934, pp. 254-71.

152. Sandberg-Vavalà, E. Review of Garrison, *Italian Romanesque Panel Painting*, *Burlington Magazine*, XCI, 1949, p. 115.

153. Sandberg-Vavalà, E. *Sienese Studies. The Development of the School of Painting of Siena*, Florence, 1953.

154. Seroux d'Agincourt, J. B. L. G. *Histoire de l'art par ses monumens, depuis sa decadence au IVe siècle jusqu'à son renouvellement au XIVe*, Paris, 1823, 6 vols.

155. Shorr, D. *The Christ Child in Devotional Images in Italy During the Fourteenth Century*, New York, 1954.

156. Siena. *Catalogo delle tavole dell' antica scuola senese riordinate nel corrente anno 1842 ed esistenti nell' I. e R. istituto di belle arti di Siena*, ed. C. Pini, Siena, 1842.

157. Siena. R. Istituto Provinciale di Belle Arti. *Catalogo della galleria*, ed. G. Milanesi, Siena, 1852.

158. Siena. R. Istituto Provinciale di Belle Arti. *Catalogo della galleria*, ed. O. Porri, Siena, 1864.

159. Siena. *Catalogo della galleria del R. istituto provinciale di belle arti di Siena*, Siena, 1872.

160. Siena. *Catalogo della galleria del R. istituto provinciale di belle arti di Siena*, Siena, 1895.

161. Siena. *Catalogo della galleria del R. istituto provinciale di belle arti in Siena*, Siena, 1903.

162. Siena. *Catalogo della galleria del R. istituto provinciale di belle arti in Siena*, Siena, 1909.

163. Siena. *La Galleria di Siena*, ed. Dami, Florence, 1924.

164. Siena. La Regia Pinacoteca di Siena. *Catalogo*, ed. C. Brandi, Rome, 1933.

165. Siena. *Guida della Pinacoteca di Siena*, ed. E. Carli, Milan, 1958.

166. Siena. *Mostra dell' antica arte senese, 1904, catalogo generale*, Siena, 1904.

167. Sinibaldi, G. and Brunetti, G., eds. *Pittura italiana del duecento e trecento. Catalogo della mostra giottesca di Firenze del 1937*, Florence, 1943.

168. Sirén, O. *A Descriptive Catalogue of the Pictures in the Jarves Collection Belonging to Yale University*, New Haven, 1916.

169. Sirén, O. "The Earliest Pictures in the Jarves Collection at Yale University," *Art in America*, III, 1915, pp. 273-83.

170. Sirén, O. in New York, Kleinberger Galleries. *Catalogue. Loan Exhibition of Italian Primitives*, New York, 1917.

171. Sirén, O. *Toskanische Maler im XIII. Jahrhundert*, Berlin, 1922.

172. Smith, M. T. "The Use of Grisaille as a Lenten Observance," *Marsyas*, VIII, 1959, pp. 43-54.

173. Stout, G. "A Puzzling Piece of Gold Leaf Tooling," Harvard University, *Fogg Art Museum Notes*, II, Cambridge, 1929, pp. 141-52.

174. Strzygowski, J. *Cimabue und Rom: Funde und Forschungen zur Kunstgeschichte und zur Topographie der Stadt Rom*, Vienna, 1888.

175. Stubblebine, J. H. "An Altarpiece by Guido da Siena," *Art Bulletin*, XLI, 1959, pp. 260-68.

176. Stubblebine, J. H. "The Development of the Throne in Dugento Tuscan Painting," *Marsyas*, VII, 1957, pp. 25-39.

177. Sturgis, R., Jr. *Manual of the Jarves Collection of Early Italian Pictures*, New Haven, 1868.

178. Thode, H. *Franz von Assisi und die Anfaenge der Kunst der Renaissance in Italien*, Berlin, 1885.

179. Thode, H. "Guido von Siena und die toscanische Malerei des 13. Jahrhunderts," *Repertorium fuer Kunstwissenschaft*, 1890, XIII, pp. 2-24.

180. Thode, H. "Sind uns Werke von Cimabue erhalten?", *Repertorium fuer Kunstwissenschaft*, XIII, 1890, pp. 25-38.

181. Toesca, P. "Guido da Siena," *Enciclopedia italiana di scienze, lettere ed arti*, XVIII, Milan, 1933, pp. 255-56.

182. Toesca, P. *Storia dell' arte italiana*, Turin, 1927.

183. Touring Club Italiano. *Guida d'Italia*, III, *Italia centrale*, Milan, 1923.

184. Touring Club Italiano. *Guida d'Italia, Toscana*, Milan, 1935.

185. Ugurgieri Azzolini, I. *Le pompe Sanesi o' vero relazione delli huomini, e donne illustri di Siena e suo stato*, Pistoia, 1649, 2 vols.

186. Utrecht. Centraal Museum, Archiepiscopal Collection. *Catalogue of Paintings*, Utrecht, 1933.

187. Vasari, G. *Le vite de' più eccellenti pittori, scultori, ed architettori* (1568), ed. G. Milanesi, Florence, 1878-1906, 9 vols.

188. Venturi, A. *Storia dell' arte italiana*, Milan, 1901-39, 11 vols.

189. Venturi, L. *Italian Paintings in America*, New York, 1933.

190. Vita, A. "La Pinacoteca d'Arezzo," *Rassegna d'arte*, xv, 1915, pp. 77-78.

191. Weigelt, C. *Duccio di Buoninsegna, Studien zur Geschichte der fruehsienesischen Tafelmalerei*, Leipzig, 1911.

192. Weigelt, C. "Guido da Siena," in Thieme, U. and Becker, F., eds., *Allgemeines Lexikon der Bildenden Kuenstler von der Antike bis zur Gegenwart*, Leipzig, 1907-50, 37 vols., vol. xv, 1922, pp. 280-84.

193. Weigelt, C. "Guido da Siena's Great Ancona: A Reconstruction," *Burlington Magazine*, LIX, 1931, pp. 15-22.

194. Weigelt, C. *Sienese Painting of the Trecento*, New York [1930].

195. Weigelt, C. "Ueber die 'muetterliche' Madonna in der italienischen Malerei des XIII Jahrhunderts," *Art Studies*, VI, 1928, pp. 195-221.

196. Wellesley, Wellesley College. *Catalogue of European and American Sculpture, Paintings and Drawings at Wellesley College*, C. Shell, and J. McAndrew, eds. Wellesley, Massachusetts, 1958.

197. White, J. "The Date of 'The Legend of St. Francis' at Assisi," *Burlington Magazine*, xcviii, 1956, pp. 344-51.

198. Wickhoff, H. "Ueber die Zeit des Guido von Siena," Institut fuer Oesterreichische Geschichtsforschung, *Mitteilungen*, 1889, x, pp. 244-86.

199. Zdekauer, L. "Cronaca," *Bullettino senese di storia patria*, xiii, 1906, pp. 255-58.

INDEX

INDEX

ILLUSTRATIONS

1. Guido da Siena, Reliquary Shutters No. 4, Siena
Pinacoteca, present exhibition (Cat. No. I)

2. Original arrangement of Reliquary Shutters (Fig. 1)

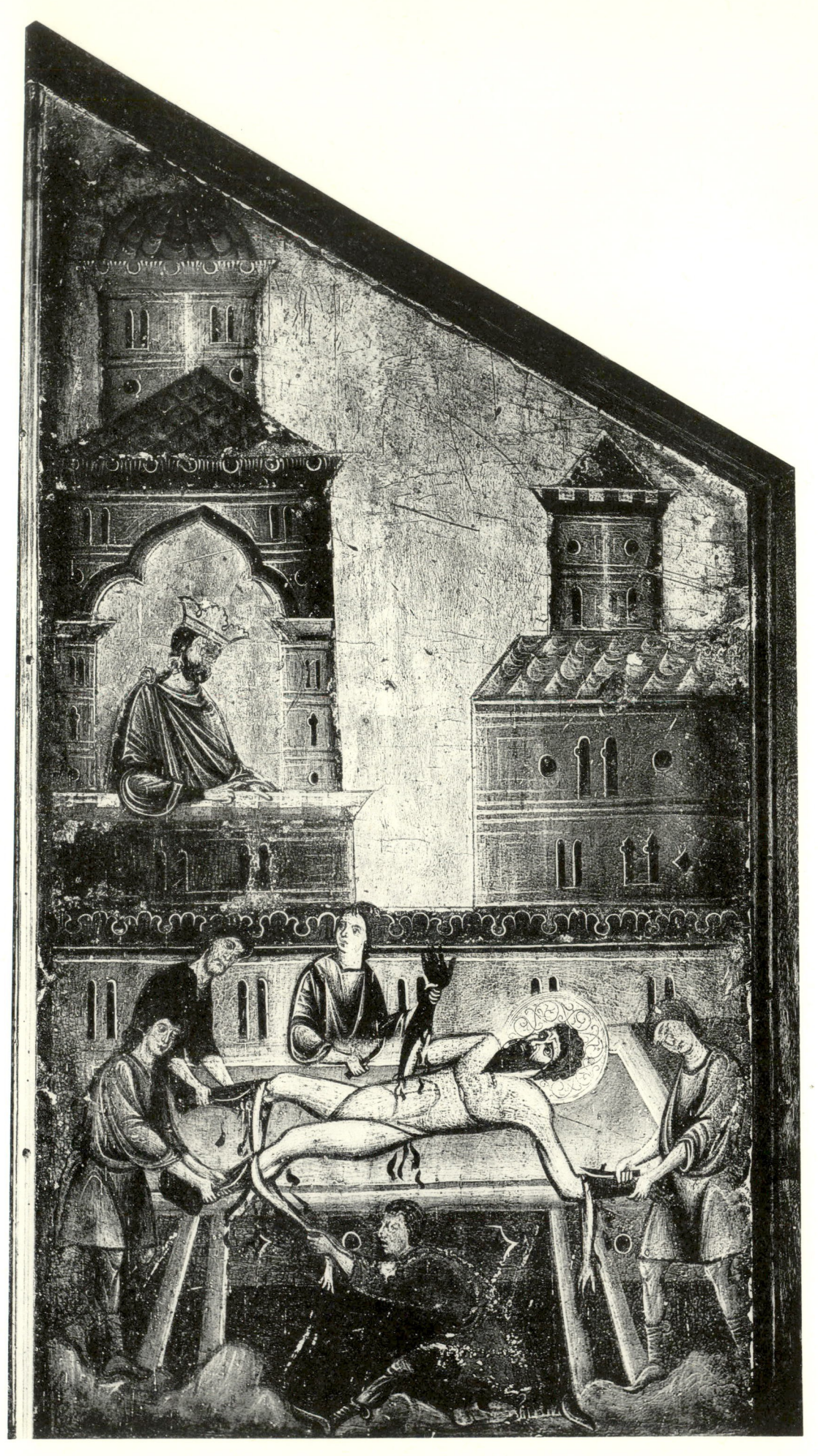

3. Guido da Siena, *Martyrdom of St. Bartholomew*, detail of Reliquary Shutters, Siena Pinacoteca (Cat. No. I)

4. Guido da Siena, *Stigmatization of St. Francis*, detail of Reliquary Shutters, Siena Pinacoteca (Cat. No. I)

5. Guido da Siena, *Martyrdom of St. Catherine of Alexandria*, detail of Reliquary Shutters,
Siena Pinacoteca (Cat. No. I)

6. Guido da Siena, *St. Clare Repulsing the Saracens*, detail of Reliquary Shutters,
Siena Pinacoteca (Cat. No. I)

7. Guido da Siena, Polyptych No. 7: *Madonna and Child with Four Saints,*
Siena Pinacoteca (Cat. No. II)

8-9. Details of Polyptych (Fig. 7)

11. *Transfiguration*, detail of Lenten Hanging (Fig. 10)

9a. Reconstruction of Polyptych No. 7 (Fig. 7)

10. Guido da Siena, Lenten Hanging, Siena Pinacoteca (Cat. No. III)

13. *Raising of Lazarus*, detail of Lenten Hanging (Fig. 10)

12. *Entry into Jerusalem*, detail of Lenten Hanging (Fig. 10)

14. Guido da Siena, Palazzo Pubblico *Madonna*, Palazzo Pubblico,
Siena (Cat. No. IVa)

15. Guido da Siena, Pediment: *Redeemer and Angels*, Palazzo Pubblico, Siena (Cat. No. IVb)

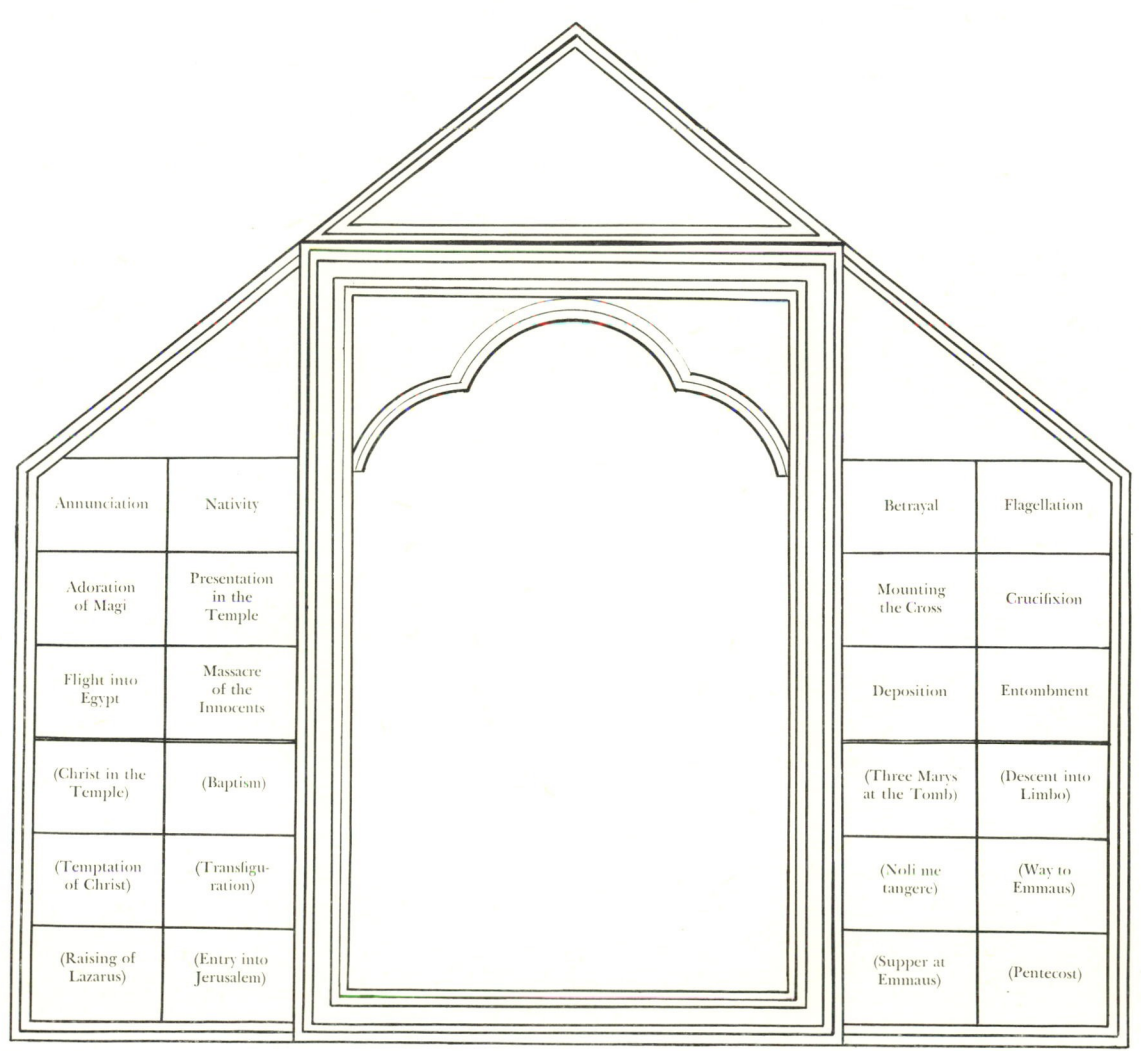

Annunciation	Nativity		Betrayal	Flagellation
Adoration of Magi	Presentation in the Temple		Mounting the Cross	Crucifixion
Flight into Egypt	Massacre of the Innocents		Deposition	Entombment
(Christ in the Temple)	(Baptism)		(Three Marys at the Tomb)	(Descent into Limbo)
(Temptation of Christ)	(Transfiguration)		(Noli me tangere)	(Way to Emmaus)
(Raising of Lazarus)	(Entry into Jerusalem)		(Supper at Emmaus)	(Pentecost)

16. Reconstruction of Guido da Siena's San Domenico Altarpiece (Cat. No. IV)

17. Angels of left spandrel, detail of Palazzo Pubblico *Madonna* (Fig. 14)

18. Guido da Siena, *Annunciation*, Princeton University Art Museum,
Princeton, New Jersey (Cat. No. IVc-1)

19. Angels of right spandrel, detail of Palazzo Pubblico *Madonna* (Fig. 14)

20. Guido da Siena, *Nativity*, Strolin Collection, Paris (Cat. No. IVc-2)

21. Guido da Siena, *Adoration of the Magi*, Lindenau Museum,
Altenburg (Cat. No. IVc-3)

22. Guido da Siena, *Flight into Egypt*, Lindenau Museum,
Altenburg (Cat. No. IVc-5)

23. Guido da Siena, *Presentation in the Temple*, Strolin Collection, Paris (Cat. No. IVc-4)

24. Guido da Siena, *Massacre of the Innocents*, Siena Pinacoteca (Cat. No. IVc-6)

25. Guido da Siena, assisted, *Betrayal*, Siena Pinacoteca
(Cat. No. IVc-7)

26. Guido da Siena, assisted, *Mounting of the Cross*, Centraal Museum, Archiepiscopal
Collection, Utrecht (Cat. No. IVc-9)

27. Guido da Siena, assisted, *Flagellation*, Lindenau Museum, Altenburg (Cat. No. IVc-8)

28. Guido da Siena, assisted, *Crucifixion*, Siena Pinacoteca (Cat. No. IVc-10)

29. Guido da Siena, assisted, *Deposition*, Siena Pinacoteca (Cat. No. IVc-11)

30. Guido da Siena, assisted, *Entombment*, Siena Pinacoteca (Cat. No. IVc-12)

31. San Bernardino Master, San Bernardino *Madonna*, Siena
Pinacoteca (Cat. No. V)

32. Assistant of Guido, Arezzo *Madonna*, Arezzo Pinacoteca
(Cat. No. VI)

33. Madonna del Voto Master, Polyptych No. 6: *Madonna and Child with Four Saints*,
Siena Pinacoteca (Cat. No. VII)

34. Clarisse Master, *Lord and Virgin Enthroned*, Clarisse Convent, Siena (Cat. No. VIII)

35. St. Peter Master, Gallerani Reliquary Shutters,
Siena Pinacoteca (Cat. No. IX)

36. *Blessed Gallerani Receiving Pilgrims*, exterior of Gallerani
Reliquary Shutters (Cat. No. IX)

37. Madonna del Voto Master, *Madonna del Voto*, Siena Cathedral (Cat. No. X)

38. Reconstruction of a Polyptych with *Madonna del Voto*

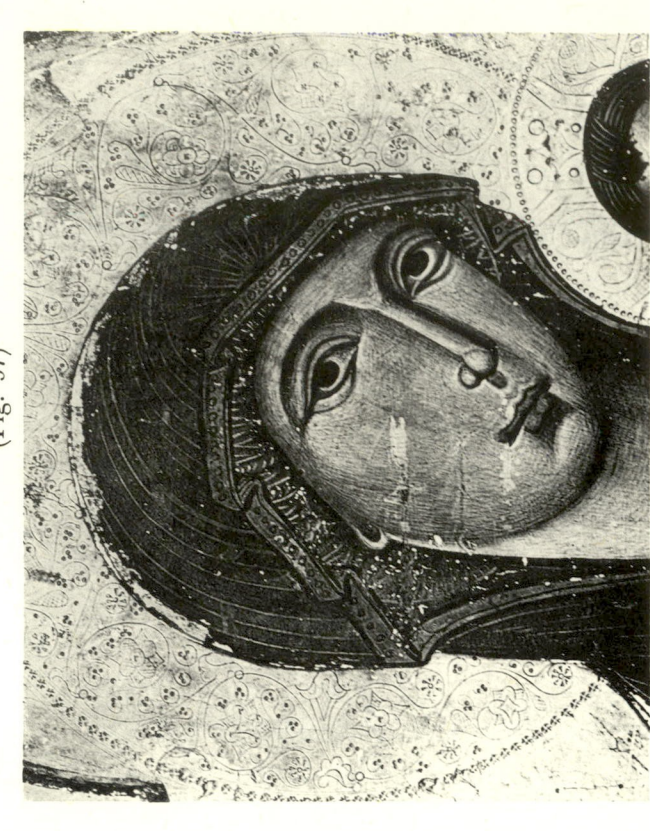

40. Madonna del Voto Master, detail of *Madonna del Voto* (Fig. 37)

41. Madonna del Voto Master, Madonna and Child, detail of Polyptych No. 6 (Cat. No. VII)

39. Madonna del Voto Master, Florence *Madonna*, Florence Academy (Cat. No. XI)

43. Assistant of Guido, Galli-Dunn *Madonna*, Siena Pinacoteca (Cat. No. XIII)

42. San Bernardino Master, Princeton *Madonna*, Princeton University Art Museum, Princeton, New Jersey (Cat. No. XII)

44. Assistant of Guido, *Coronation of the Virgin*, Courtauld Institute of Art, London (Cat. No. XIV)

45. The Lord and Virgin, detail of *Coronation of the Virgin* (Fig. 44)

46-47. Heads of Angels, details of *Coronation of the Virgin* (Fig. 44)

48. Assistant of Guido, *St. Dominic,* Fogg Art Museum, Harvard University, Cambridge, Massachusetts (Cat. No. XV)

49. St. Peter Master, *Last Judgment*, Museo Diocesano d'Arte Sacra, Grosseto (Cat. No. XVI)

50. Clarisse Master, Polyptych: *Madonna and Child with Four Saints*, Brooks Memorial Art Gallery, Kress Collection, Memphis, Tennessee (Cat. No. XVII). Before restoration

51. Memphis Polyptych after restoration

52. Assistant of Guido, *Crucifixion*, Yale University Art Gallery, James Jackson Jarves Collection,
New Haven, Connecticut (Cat. No. XVIII)

53. St. Peter Master, St. Peter Altarpiece, Siena Pinacoteca (Cat. No. XIX)

55. Clarisse Master, Crucifix,
Galleria del Palazzo Comunale,
San Gimignano (Cat. No. XXI)

54. St. Peter Master, Montaione *Madonna*,
San Regolo, Montaione (Cat. No. XX)

56. Clarisse Master, Tabernacle, National Museum, Czartoryski Collection, Kraków (Cat. No. XXII). After restoration

57. Madonna and Child, detail of Tabernacle (Fig. 56). Before restoration

58. *Entombment* and *Crucifixion*, details of Tabernacle (Fig. 56). Before restoration

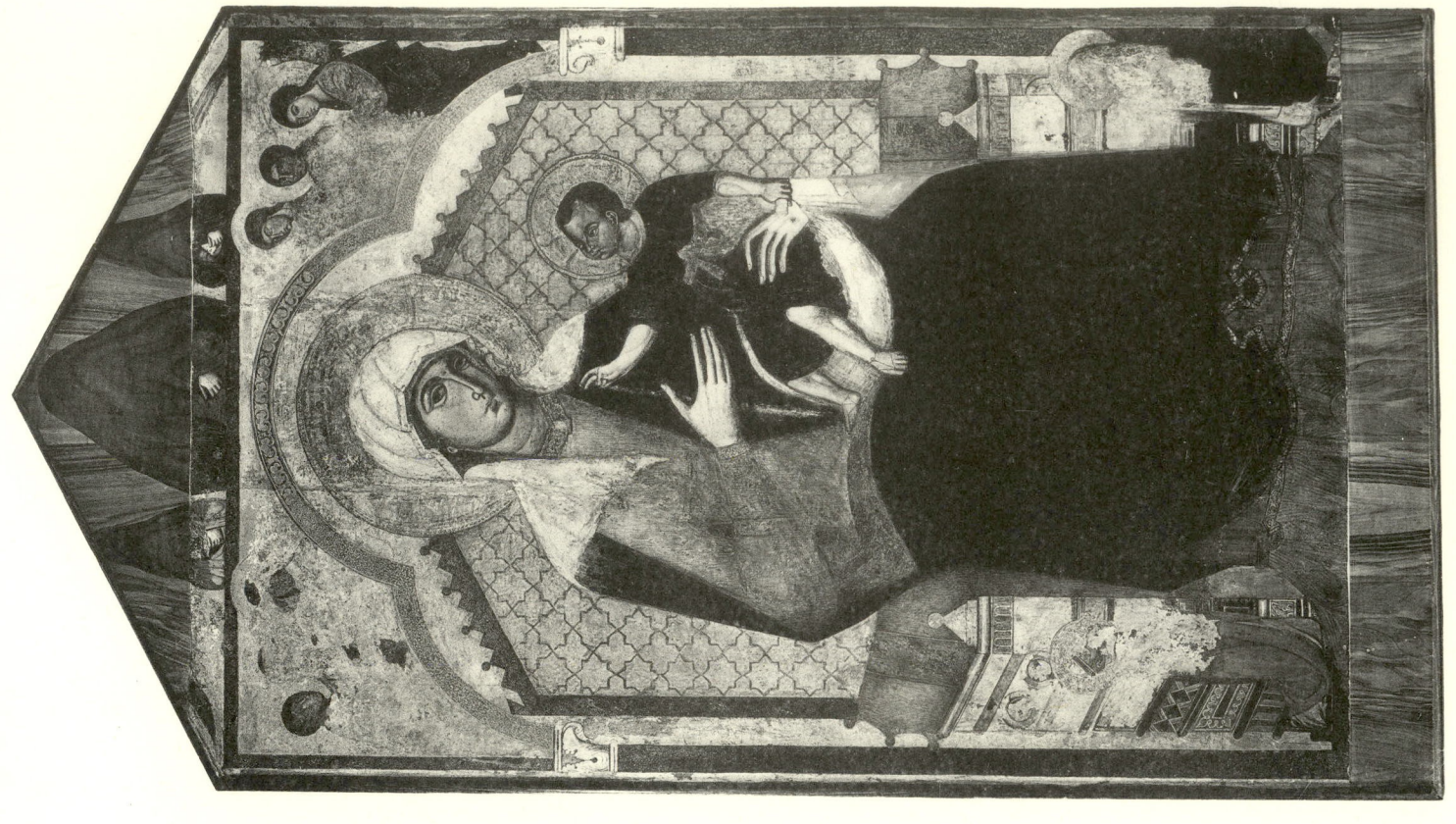

60. Follower of Guido, San Gimignano *Madonna*, Galleria del Palazzo Comunale, San Gimignano (Cat. No. XXIV)

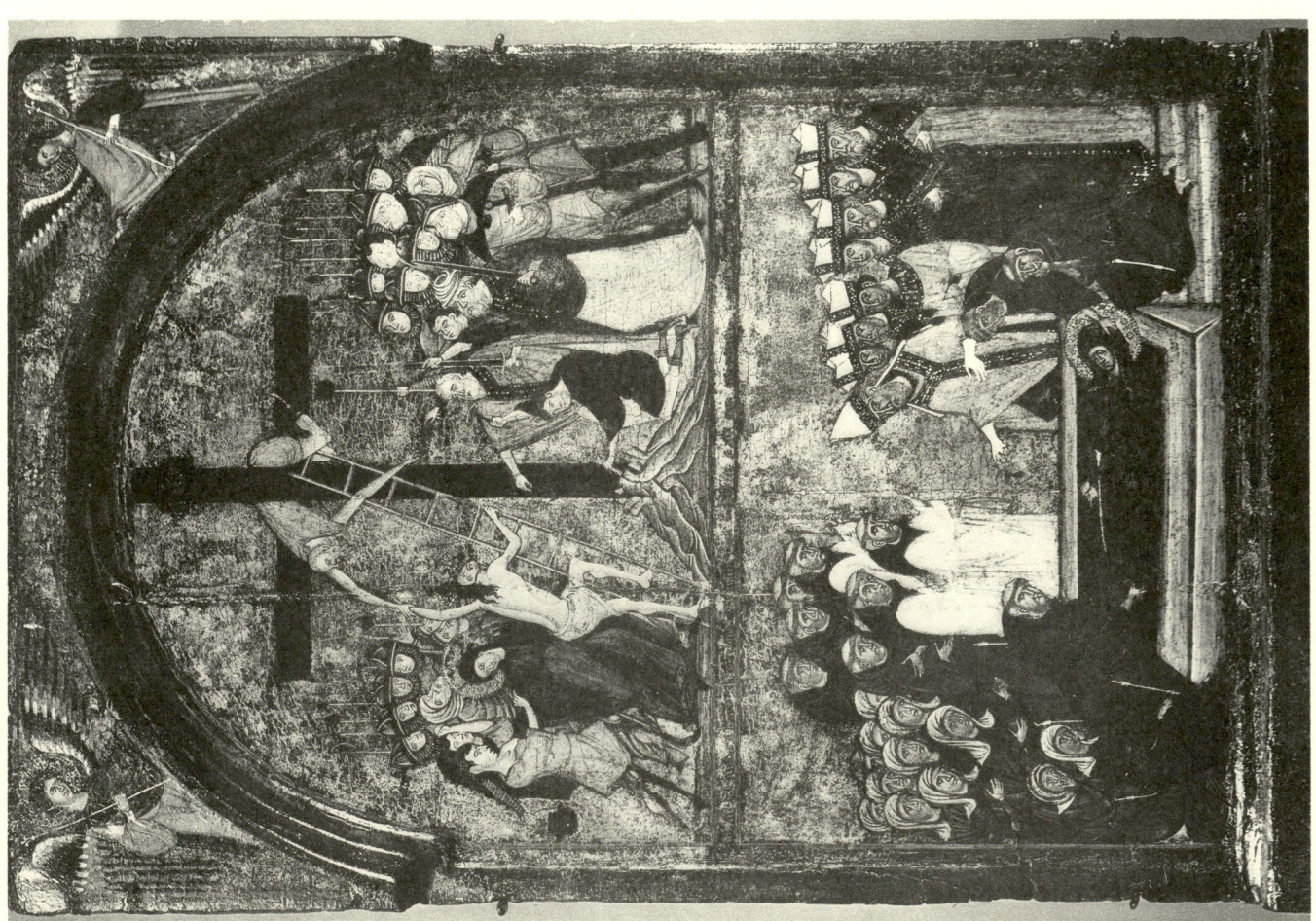

59. Follower of Guido, Tabernacle Center, Wellesley College Museum, Wellesley Massachusetts (Cat. No. XXIII)

61. Follower of Guido, St. Francis Altarpiece, Siena
Pinacoteca (Cat. No. XXV)

62. Bonaventura Berlinghieri, St. Francis Altarpiece,
San Francesco, Pescia

63-64. Bonaventura Berlinghieri, details of St. Francis Altarpiece (Fig. 62)

65. Guido da Siena, detail of left spandrel angels from Palazzo Pubblico *Madonna* (Cat. No. IVa)

66. Guido da Siena, Christ Child, detail of Polyptych No. 7 (Cat. No. II)

67. Guido da Siena, detail of *Entry into Jerusalem* from the Lenten Hanging (Cat. No. III)

68. Guido da Siena, Head of Redeemer, detail of Palazzo Pubblico Pediment (Cat. No. IVb)

69. Guido da Siena, St. Francis, detail of Polyptych No. 7 (Cat. No. II)

71. Guido da Siena, Right side of throne, detail of Palazzo Pubblico *Madonna* (Cat. No. IVa)

70. Guido da Siena, Left side of throne, detail of Palazzo Pubblico *Madonna* (Cat. No. IVa)

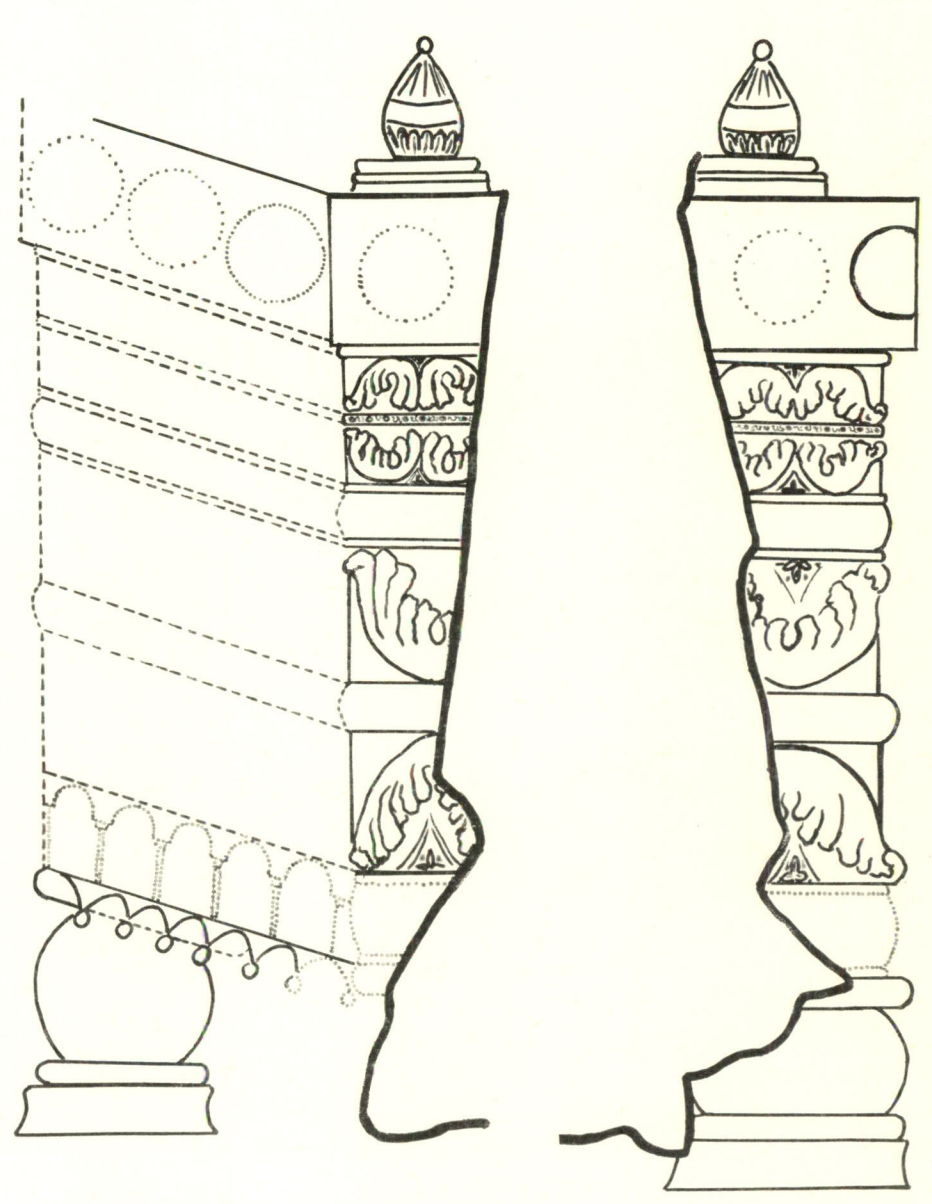

72. Cimabue, *Madonna with St. Francis*, detail, Lower Church, Assisi

73. Reconstruction of the sides of the throne of the Palazzo Pubblico
Madonna (Cat. No. IVa and Fig. 14)

74. Meliore da Toscana, Polyptych, Uffizi, Florence

75. Vigoroso da Siena, Polyptych, Perugia Pinacoteca

76. Deodato Orlandi, Polyptych, Museo Civico, Pisa

77. Cimabue and Shop, *Angel Gallery*, transept, Upper Church, Assisi

78. Simone Martini, Polyptych, Museo Civico, Pisa

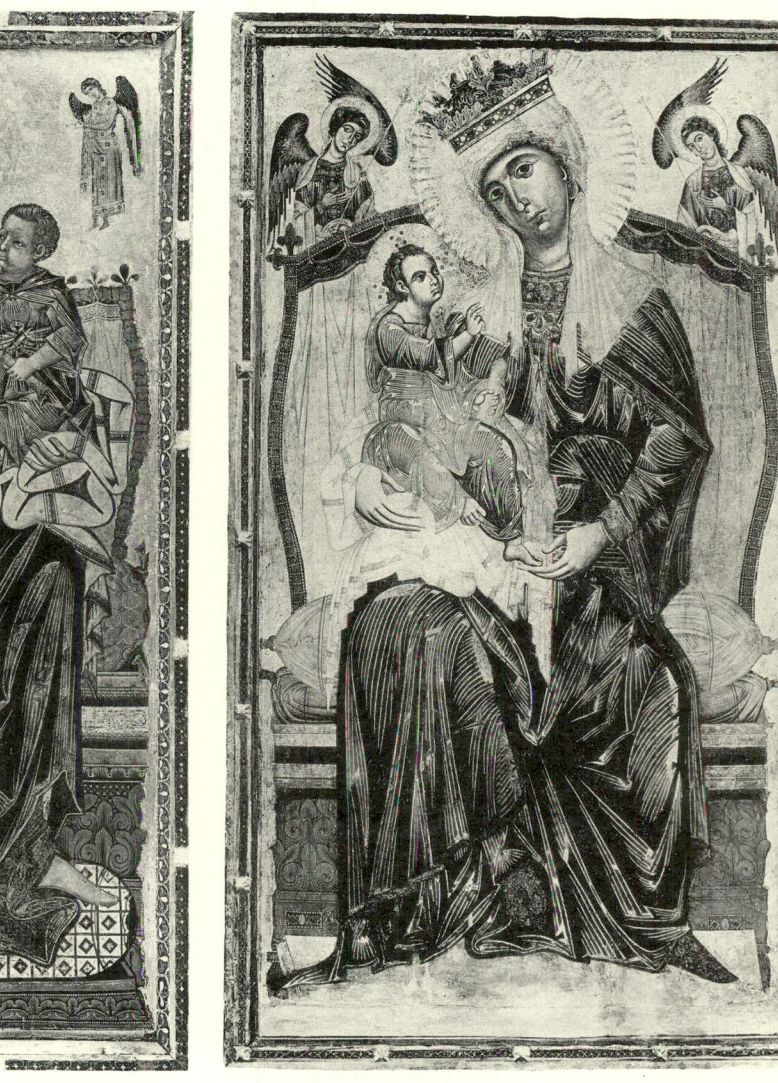

79. Sienese School, *Madonna and Child*, Opera del Duomo, Siena

80. Coppo di Marcovaldo, *Madonna and Child*, Santa Maria dei Servi, Siena

81. Coppo di Marcovaldo, *Madonna and Child*, Santa Maria dei Servi, Orvieto

83. Guido da Siena, Pediment: *Redeemer and Angels*, Palazzo Pubblico, Siena (Cat. No. IVb)

82. Lucchese School, *Cimasa* of Crucifix, Santa Maria, Tereglio

84. Scenes from the Lives of Christ and the Baptist, cupola mosaic, Florence Baptistery

85. Scenes from the Lives of Christ and the Baptist, cupola mosaic, Florence Baptistery

86. Scenes from the Lives of Christ and the Baptist, cupola mosaic, Florence Baptistery

87. Nicola Pisano, *Adoration of the Magi*, detail of the
Siena Pulpit, Siena Cathedral

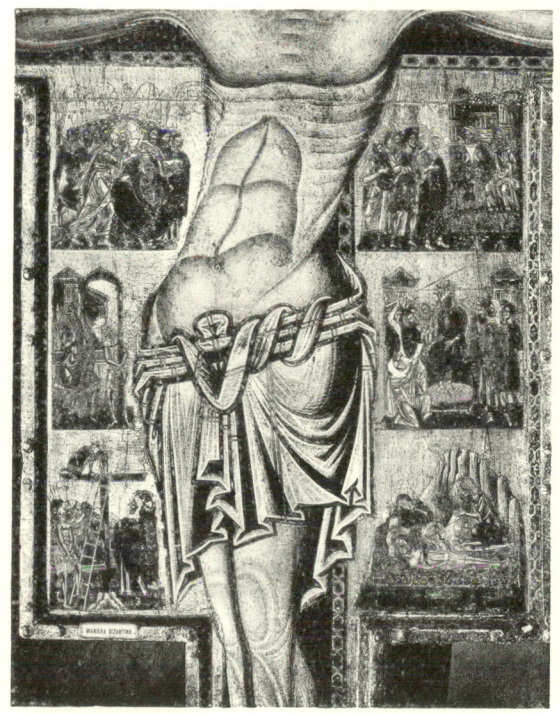

88. Coppo di Marcovaldo, Passion Scenes,
detail of Crucifix, Galleria del
Palazzo Comunale, San Gimignano

89. Cimabue, *Crucifixion*, left transept,
Upper Church, Assisi

90. Umbrian School, Tabernacle, Perugia Pinacoteca

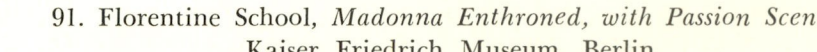

91. Florentine School, *Madonna Enthroned, with Passion Scenes,*
Kaiser Friedrich Museum, Berlin

95. Cimabue, *Virgin in Glory*, choir, Upper Church, Assisi

92. San Bernardino Master, detail of
San Bernardino *Madonna* (Cat. No. V)

93. San Bernardino Master, detail of
Princeton *Madonna* (Cat. No. XII)

94. Guido da Siena, Madonna, detail
of Polyptych No. 7 (Cat. No. II)

96. School of Cimabue, *Madonna and Child*,
Acton Collection, Florence

97. School of Cimabue, *Madonna and Child*,
San Remigio, Florence

98. School of Cimabue, *Madonna and Child*,
Galleria Sabauda, Turin

99. School of Cimabue, *Madonna and Child*,
Sant'Andrea, Mosciano

100. St. Peter Master, *Stigmatization*, detail of the Gallerani Reliquary Shutters (Cat. No. IX)

101. Guido da Siena, *Stigmatization*, detail of Reliquary Shutters No. 4 (Cat. No. I)

102. St. Peter Master, *Blessed Gallerani Praying*, detail of the Gallerani Reliquary Shutters (Cat. No. IX)

103. Guido da Siena, detail of *Crucifixion* (Cat. No. IVc-10)

104. Berlinghiero, *Madonna and Child*, Collection of
Mrs. J. I. Straus, New York City

105. St. Francis Master, "Pallet" of
St. Francis, Santa Maria degli
Angeli, Assisi

106. Jacopo Torriti, *Dormition and Coronation of the Virgin*,
apse mosaic, Santa Maria Maggiore, Rome

107. Tuscan School, *Ascension*, façade mosaic, San Frediano, Lucca

108. Christ from *Last Judgment*, cupola mosaic, Florence Baptistery

109. School of Berlinghiero, Tabernacle, Stoclet Collection, Brussels

110. Nicola Pisano, *Crucifixion*, detail of Siena Pulpit, Siena Cathedral

111. St. Peter Master, *Annunciation*, detail of St. Peter Altarpiece (Cat. No. XIX)

112. St. Peter Master, *Calling of Peter*, detail of St. Peter Altarpiece (Cat. No. XIX)

113. St. Peter Master, detail of Grosseto *Last Judgment* (Cat. No. XVI)

114. St. Peter Master, *Blessed Gallerani
Distributing Alms*, detail of the
Gallerani Reliquary Shutters
(Cat. No. IX)

115. St. Peter Master, *St. Peter Led from Prison*,
detail of St. Peter Altarpiece
(Cat. No. XIX)

116. Guido da Siena, detail of *Crucifixion* (Cat. No. IVc-10)

117. Duccio, detail of *Crucifixion* from the *Maestà*, Opera del Duomo, Siena

118. Deodato Orlandi, Crucifix, dated 1288, Lucca Pinacoteca

119. Deodato Orlandi, Crucifix, dated 1301, Convent of St. Clare, San Miniato al Tedesco

120. St. Peter Master, detail of *Blessed Gallerani Praying before a Crucifix* from the Gallerani Reliquary Shutters (Cat. No. IX)

121. Clarisse Master, *Cimasa*
of the San Gimignano Cross (Cat. No. XXI)

122. Clarisse Master, Madonna and Child,
detail of Memphis Polyptych (Cat. No. XVII)

123. Clarisse Master, detail of *Lord and Virgin Enthroned* (Cat. No. VIII)

126. Cimabue, Trinita *Madonna*, Uffizi, Florence

125. Duccio, Rucellai *Madonna*, Uffizi, Florence

124. Bardi St. Francis Master, St. Francis Altarpiece, Bardi Chapel, Santa Croce, Florence

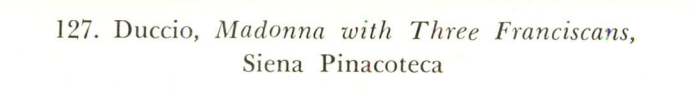

127. Duccio, *Madonna with Three Franciscans*,
Siena Pinacoteca

128. Duccio, Tabernacle, London National Gallery